COUNTRY ALES AND BREWERIES

Country Ales
and Breweries

Text by Roger Protz
Photography by Steve Sharples

WEIDENFELD & NICOLSON
LONDON

First published in Great Britain in 1999 by Weidenfeld & Nicolson

Text copyright © Roger Protz, 1999
Photographs copyright © Steve Sharples, 1999

The moral right of Roger Protz to be identified as the author of this work has been
asserted in accordance with the Copyright, Designs and Patents Act of 1988
Design and layout copyright © Weidenfeld & Nicolson, 1999

A CIP catalogue record for this book is available from the British Library.

ISBN 0 297 83625 0

Designed by Nigel Soper

Printed in Italy by Printer Trento srl.

ENDPAPERS: HOBSONS BREWERY, SHROPSHIRE
HALF TITLE: HOBSONS BREWERY, SHROPSHIRE
TITLE PAGE: KENT OAST HOUSES

Weidenfeld & Nicolson
The Orion Publishing Group
Orion House
5 Upper St Martin's Lane
London WC2H 9EA

CONTENTS

INTRODUCTION

They sell good beer at Haslemere
And under Guildford Hill.
At little Cowfold as I've been told
A beggar may drink his fill:
There is a good brew in Amberley too,
And by the bridge also;
But the swipes[1] they take in at the Washington Inn
Is the very best Beer I know.
HILAIRE BELLOC

ALL HANDS TO THE PUMPS

Beers from Adnams of Southwold in Suffolk, brewers of classic country beers with a hint of salt and seaweed due to the brewery's proximity to the North Sea. Brewing water used to be pumped from a well under the sea until it became contaminated. Adnams now uses the public water supply.

IT WAS ONLY IN COMPARATIVELY recent times, with the rush to industrialize Britain, that brewing moved from being a country pursuit to an urban one. Land enclosures drove rural people into the towns. As towns grew and factories, mines, foundries, mills and shipyards appeared, commercial brewers set up in business to meet the insatiable thirsts of the new urban masses. Today, as industry recedes and scores of small craft brewers fire their mash tuns and coppers in rural locations, it is timely to recall that for most of the recorded history of the British Isles, beer-making has had powerful bucolic roots. Even when the great eighteenth-century entrepreneurial brewers, such as Sam Whitbread, were stamping their mark on London with their new, mass-produced porter beers, they challenged at the same time the hegemony of the powerful gentrified country brewers who continued their slower practice of making 'vatted' ales that matured for a year or more in giant wooden tuns.

Centuries earlier, Iron Age Celts in Britain made a grain-based drink called curmi. Barley and other cereals were brought to the British Isles by the sea-trading Phoenicians who also instructed the natives on the craft of ale-making that dated from at least 3000 BC in Ancient Egypt, Babylon and Mesopotamia. As the Romans marched north they found that the tribes in the lands that were to become Britain, France, Germany and Spain, made a potent and potable alcohol that was an acceptable replacement for wine when supplies ran out. Pliny recorded that, 'the nations of the west have their own intoxicant from grain soaked in water;

1 *Nineteenth-century term for cheap beer.*

GRIST TO THE MILL

Malt, say brewers, is the soul of beer. Tuckers Maltings in Newton Abbot, Devon, is one of the last traditional 'floor maltings' in Britain. Most malt is now made in rotating metal drums but at Tuckers the barley is laid out on heated floors, where it starts to germinate. The 'green' or unfinished malt is then cured or gently roasted in a kiln. The temperatures used produce malts of different colours: all beers are made mainly from pale malt, rich in natural enzymes, with darker malts added for colour and flavour.

there are many ways of making it in Gaul and Spain and under different names, though the principle is the same'. The Emperor Julian was less impressed. After his first taste of British curmi he penned a short poem titled 'On Wine Made from Barley':

Who made you and from what?
By the true Bacchus I know you not.
He smells of nectar
But you smell of goat.

If the Romans were ambivalent about beer, the Anglo-Saxons who invaded the British Isles following the Roman withdrawal had no such inhibitions. Öl or ealu, from which came the English word ale, was a vital and essential part of the Anglo-Saxon life and culture. Paradise for the Saxons was a great hall where the dead passed their time drinking ale while in the real world ale or malt were used to pay fines, tolls, rents and debts.

All brewing was done in the home. It was the responsibility of the woman or 'ale wife' to ensure that the men of the household were well supplied with ale. Alreck, King of Hordoland, chose Geirhild to be his queen for the sound reason that she brewed good ale. Brewed without hops but spiced with herbs, ale was as essential as bread and was made by the hearth from the same ingredients. (Beer, from the Old German word beor, was bittered with hops and was a later development.) Typhoid and cholera were widespread. Water was foul and was safe to drink only when boiled and made sterile during the brewing process. Bread and ale, both rich in vitamin B, formed crucial elements of the early British diet.

In the course of time, some ale wives became renowned in their hamlets and villages for the quality of their ale, and people went to their homes to drink. When a new brew was ready, the ale wife would place a pole above the door and tie a branch or part of a bush to it as an invitation to her neighbours to come and imbibe. The public house and its inn sign (still recalled today in pubs called the Holly Bush) had arrived. The Norman invaders brought wine and cider with them but found ale-making deeply ingrained in the English of all classes. The Domesday Book recorded forty-three *cerevisiarii* (brewers) whose quality of ale was taken sufficiently seriously for fines to be imposed on those that did not brew to an acceptable standard. In Chester, for example, brewers of inferior ales were ducked in the town pond or fined four shillings for making bad ale – *malam cerevisiam faciens*. In 1158, Thomas à Becket took two chariot-loads of casks of ale with him on a diplomatic mission to France 'decocted from choice fat grain as a gift for the French who wondered at such an invention – a drink most wholesome, clear of all dregs, rivalling wine in colour and surpassing it in savour'. Becket, who came to an untimely end in Canterbury Cathedral, had learned his brewing skills as a young monk when he made ale for the abbot of St Albans Abbey in Hertfordshire.

Until the dissolution of the monasteries by Henry VIII between 1536 and 1540, the Church dominated brewing for several centuries. Monks built brewhouses to supply themselves and pilgrims with wholesome ale. The usual ration of beer for the monks, approved by the abbot, was a gallon a day of 'small' or weak ale. Production was prodigious. The malthouse at Fountains Abbey in Yorkshire was sixty square feet and the brewhouse produced sixty barrels of strong ale every ten days. The monks brewed the finest ale, *prima melior*, for the abbot and distinguished visitors, a second brew, *secunda*, for lay brothers and employees, and a weak *tertia* for pilgrims. The method for producing ale, which survived for many centuries, was to use just one 'mash' of grain for the entire output. The first mash would produce a strong ale, the second a common ale, and the final one a small ale considered suitable for women, children and impoverished pilgrims.

The powerful position of the Church did not weaken domestic brewing. Ale was made not only in the homes of the common people but also in the castles and mansions of the nobility. In 1512 the Northumberland Household Book recorded that the powerful Percy family, ennobled as the earls of Northumberland, consumed for breakfast during Lent 'a

DARK AND MYSTERIOUS

Morocco Ale, brewed by Daleside in
Yorkshire, recreates a mysterious and
enigmatic beer that was once made at
Levens Hall in Lancashire several
hundred years ago. The beer was stored
and matured for long periods and was
heavily spiced, recalling the time when
brewers used spices and herbs to
flavour ale before the universal adoption
of the hop.

quart of ale each for my lord and lady, two pints for my lady's gentlewoman and one and a half gallons for the gentlemen of the chapel and children'. Apart from wine and spirits, no other beverages were consumed. Tea and coffee were unheard of and water was still unsanitary: it was said at the time that 'a gentleman drank water only as a penance'. Ale-making would have been rudimentary in the homes of the country people but was more sophisticated in the castles and grand houses of the nobility, in monasteries and seats of learning. The brewhouse at Queen's College, Oxford, for example, was built in 1340 and survived until 1939. Save for the introduction of a thermometer, the brewhouse remained unchanged throughout its history. The mash tun was made of memel oak and had two outlet pipes with metal strainers through which the sweet extract would flow, leaving the used grain behind. The extract ran into another wooden vessel, the underback, below the mash tun and was then transferred by hand to an open copper, where it was boiled: hops were added at this stage when they started to be used in the brewing process. The liquid was cooled in large vessels that held 216 gallons each and was then run into a wooden fermenting 'round' where yeast was mixed in. As soon as a vigorous fermentation started, the liquid was pumped to casks in the cellar. The vigour of fermentation drove some of the yeast and liquid out of the bung holes in the casks and was collected in a trough. The yeast was saved and re-used in later brews. Once fermentation was complete, the casks were sealed and the ale was left to mature.

The arrival of the hop plant in south-east England in the fifteenth century with Dutch merchants, who came to trade in Kent and Sussex, changed the nature of brewing in England, encouraging the development of commercial or 'common' brewers in towns and cities. The hop made slow progress at first. The Brewers' Company was set up in 1437 to defend the interests of ale brewers who did not use hops and the plant was banned by the burghers of Norwich, in spite of the fact that many Flemish weavers had settled there. In 1519 the 'wicked and pernicious weed' was outlawed in Shrewsbury and Henry VIII instructed his court brewer to make ale without hops. Slowly, however, commercial brewers began to appreciate the advantages of the remarkable plant that, with its oils, acids and tannins, protected beer from bacterial infection and gave it much better keeping qualities, as well as adding a pleasing and refreshing bitterness. At a royal banquet in Windsor Park in 1528, fifteen gallons of hopped

BREWERS OVER

A BARREL

Coopering, the ancient skill of fashioning beer casks from wood, is a dying art in Britain as a result of the almost universal use of metal by brewers. Once breweries employed large armies of coopers to build and repair casks. Today just a handful of breweries still use wooden casks, usually made from imported oak. The cooper in the picture is employed by Wadworth of Devizes. A long apprenticeship is needed to become a fully-fledged cooper, during the course of which he has to learn to use the ancient tools needed to cut, carve and smooth the staves that are then held in place by metal hoops. When the apprenticeship is finished, the cooper is rolled round the brewery yard in a cask of his own making, and is tarred and feathered and liberally doused with ale.

beer and a similar quantity of unhopped ale were offered to the guests. The date suggests that Henry VIII had, by then, relaxed his opposition to the use of the hop. More significantly, the beer cost just twenty pennies, while the ale cost two shillings and sixpence (half a crown). The better keeping qualities of hopped beer meant that less malt had to be used. Ale was traditionally brewed to a high strength to prolong its life, and strength could be obtained only by using large amounts of expensive barley malt.

Reynold Scott, an Oxford graduate who farmed in Kent, argued the case for hops in his book *A Perfite Platforme for a Hoppe Garden*, published in 1574:

> *Whereas you cannot make above 8-9 gallons of indifferent ale from 1 bushel of malt, you may draw 18-20 gallons of very good beer. If your ale may endure a fortnight, your beer through the benefit of the hop shall continue a month, and what grace it yieldeth to the taste, all men may judge that have sense in their mouths.*

Scott's book ran to three editions. With the aid of woodcuts, he described the way to prepare the soil and to erect poles as soon as the hops appeared above the ground. The rich soil in Kent was ideally suited for hop growing, early land enclosure offered protection to farmers, and there was an abundance of wood for making poles and charcoal for fires to dry the hops.

The profitable advantages of hopped beer were not lost on brewers. Brewing was still largely confined to the home or to ale houses where landlords brewed for consumption on the premises. But the growing towns were crammed with ale houses, taverns and inns. A census of 1577 showed there were 19,759 public drinking places in England and Wales and with a population of 3,700,00, this meant there was a drinking outlet for every 187 people. Demand for ale and beer was beginning to outstrip supply in the towns. Commercial brewers hurried to meet the demand and they used hops to flavour and protect beer as well as making the product more profitable. By the middle of the sixteenth century there were twenty-six 'common brewers' in London, most of them based in Southwark, conveniently close to the hop market at the Borough where hops from Kent were sold. Fifty years later London had 194 commercial brewers.

Hops began to transform the way in which beer was made. But Britain was still a mainly agricultural society and it took time for the hop to be adopted in rural communities. Of course, hops were grown in the country but Kent was an isolated area. News travelled slowly and came mainly from the pulpit during the Sunday sermon and it is unlikely that many clerics advised the brewers among their flocks to adopt the hop as part of their brewing practice. Domestic brewers were unwilling to change their methods or to go to the expense of adding to their rudimentary equipment while commercial country brewers scorned the fast ways of the 'vulgar' towns. Far from waning, the power of country brewers waxed in the eighteenth century. In 1734 an important book on brewing technique, *The London and Country Brewer*, ran to nine editions, advised brewers on the need for cleanliness and sterilizing of casks, and referred to pale malts cured in kilns fired by coke. Until this time, all brewing malt had been kilned over wood fires. Coal was taxed and was difficult to mine, while wood was not taxed and was found in abundance in the great woods and forests that still covered much of the land. Coal also gave off noxious gases that infected malt with unpleasant flavours, was banned in towns and cities as it created choking fogs and was too expensive to produce for urban brewers, most of whom were quite modest in size. (Ralph Harwood, the London brewer who is said to have invented porter beer around 1722, produced a modest 20,000 barrels of beer a year in his Bell Brewhouse in Shoreditch. A century later the great London porter brewers, such as Whitbread, Barclay Perkins, Meux Reid and Truman Hanbury, were making between 120,000 and 270,000 barrels a year.)

But pale malt was an important development. Wood-cured malt was not just brown but was frequently scorched and many of the natural enzymes in the malt were destroyed. The enzymes convert starch into fermentable sugars during the mashing process, and brown malt had a low 'diastatic power' compared to the new coke-kilned pale malts that were rich in enzymes. Brewers also needed less pale malt than brown to make beer, an important consideration as commercial brewing developed.

The power of the country brewers, often wealthy landowners who brewed as a sideline to their farming, grew as the eighteenth century brought with it a craze in London for a beer called 'three threads' or 'three thirds' which was a blend of pale, brown and 'stale' ale. Pale ale

GOING WITH THE GRAIN

The Langley Maltings in Smethwick, West Midlands, are owned by Wolverhampton and Dudley Breweries, Britain's biggest regional brewer. As at Tuckers in Newton Abbot, the grain is 'floor malted' – spread over heated floors – rather than germinated in rotating metal drums. Most brewers buy grain from specialist maltsters but Wolverhampton and Dudley prefers to make its own malt as it believes the combination of Maris Otter barley and the floor method produces the sweetest and silkiest grain for brewing and makes for a delightful biscuity and juicy maltiness in the finished beer.
The group is best known for its Banks's Mild and Bitter beers produced in Wolverhampton.

and stale were both sold to the London brewers by country brewers. Stale was brown beer, made in London but sent to country brewers to mature for a year or more in large oak vessels called tuns. During this long conditioning, wild yeasts and micro-flora in the vats gave the beer a lactic tang that was much appreciated by drinkers at the time. The small, cramped London breweries did not have the space to build large conditioning tuns and were happy for country brewers to do the work for them, although they were less happy at the high prices charged.

The authority of the country brewers came under sustained attack when Ralph Harwood produced a beer he called 'entire butt' that replicated the taste of three threads but came from just one cask or butt, avoiding the need for blending in the pub cellar. The beer became so popular that while the style was not mentioned in *The London and Country Brewer* in 1734, H. Jackson's *Essay on Bread* in 1758 reported that 'Beer, commonly call'd Porter, is become almost the universal cordial of the populace.' Porter was the nickname given to entire butt as a result of its popularity among London street-market porters, and within a few years the nickname had become the style. The demand for porter and its strongest or stoutest version, stout, was so insatiable that small brewers such as Sam Whitbread abandoned attempts to make pale and brown beers and built large new breweries that produced just porter and stout. Their success and wealth, allied to new technologies such as the steam engine, enabled them to make pale malt and pale ale in London, and to store and age their beers in their own breweries. Whitbread at first rented fifty-four buildings in London to store his porter but from 1760 the beer was matured in enormous underground cisterns, each one containing 4,000 barrels, beneath the Whitbread brewery in the Barbican.

FROM STRENGTH
TO STRENGTH . . .

Ballard's is a successful small or 'micro'
brewery based in an old sawmill. Run
by Carola Brown, a rare example of a
modern 'brewster', the brewery's beers
include an annual ale with a strength to
match the year. Blizzard in 1998, for
example, was 9.8 per cent alcohol.

Porter and stout, dark brown beers at first which became black with the introduction of roasted malt in the early nineteenth century, were urban beers, brewed first in London and then in Bristol, Glasgow, Edinburgh, Dublin, Belfast, Cork and other great towns and cities within the United Kingdom. The power of the country brewers was not broken by porter although they had lost their grip on the towns. But they remained a potent force and the Country Brewers' Association became a powerful lobby and a principal partner in the new Brewers' Society formed in 1904 to bring together both urban and rural producers. When porter was replaced in popularity from the mid-nineteenth century by the new India Pale Ales brewed in the small country town of Burton-on-Trent, the country brewers regained some of the authority lost to the towns. Such was the popularity of pale ale, brewed first for the colonial trade but then conveyed to all parts of Britain by the new railway system, that, for a while, the tables were turned. Brewers from London, Liverpool and Warrington went to Burton to build breweries there in order to use the hard spring waters from the Trent Valley that were essential to the production of the style. When Edward Greene, who ran Greene King in Bury St Edmunds, Suffolk, died in 1891, he was paid the following tribute by the London evening newspaper the *Star*: 'He was one of the first country brewers to discover that beer need not be a vile, black, turgid stuff, but brewed a bright amber-coloured liquid of Burton type, which he sold at a shilling per gallon and made a fortune.'

A Beer Act of 1830 that enabled any householder to obtain a one-guinea licence to sell beer proved a disaster. Most of the small, rural beer shops, nicknamed 'Tom and Jerry houses', were rough, unsavoury places run by inexperienced licensees. When most of them went bankrupt, the country brewers bought them at knockdown prices and started to build 'tied estates' of directly owned and supplied public houses. The tied pub proved an important buffer for the country brewers against the rising power of the great urban brewers who used railways, advertising and even home deliveries to build their businesses. But, inevitably, with the rise of industrial Britain, the cutting down of forests and the paving over of the countryside, country brewing declined in the nineteenth and twentieth centuries. Home brewing in stately homes and mansions was the first to go, victim not so much to industrialism as to the nobility's transfer of affection from beer to imported wine. When England was at war with France, patriotic aristocrats drank beer, often brewed in their homes, with head butlers doubling as brewers. As A. E. Housman wrote:

Oh many a peer of England brews
Livelier liquor than the Muse
And malt does more than Milton can
To justify God's ways to man.

Barley wine, strong and matured for several years, was the aristocracy's answer to the wines of the perfidious French. But when hostilities ceased and the 'Hun' was identified as a greater threat to Britain's imperial power, home brewing declined as the upper classes refreshed themselves with claret, port and sherry. Today only one stately home, Traquair House in the Scottish borders, still brews on a regular basis while occasional beer is made at Shugborough Hall in Staffordshire.

Country brewers remain and thrive in country towns and they are the prominent feature of this book. No apology is offered for the inclusion of Burton-on-Trent which may not be the prettiest town in England but, surrounded by the Trent Valley, it has played a pivotal role in the development of brewing. The large country brewers are joined in these pages by many new small craft or 'micro' brewers, recent arrivals in the 1980s and 1990s. Many were set up by keen home brewers who turned a hobby into a business, bringing much-needed choice to a country more and more dominated by a handful of beer giants who have turned their backs on tradition and quality with mass-advertised, processed products.

Country Ales and Breweries is a celebration of both an old and a renewed tradition of beer-making, and of Britain's great and singular offering to the world of beer. It is a small contribution to their appreciation and survival.

ROGER PROTZ
ST ALBANS
AUTUMN 1998

HORSE WITH

DELIGHT ...

Wadworth of Devizes in Wiltshire still delivers beer to neighbouring pubs by horse-drawn drays. The drays are a simple and effective method of promoting the brewery's beers and are more cost-effective over short journeys than diesel-fuelled lorries. Several other breweries, including Samuel Smith in Yorkshire and Young's in London, also deliver beer by horse-drawn vehicles, which are also used at shows and parades, including the Lord Mayor's Show in London.

How Beer is Brewed

BEER IS THE RESULT of turning the starches in malted barley into fermentable malt sugars, boiling the sugary extract with hops and then fermenting the liquid with yeast to produce alcohol. The brewing process starts in a maltings where barley is soaked in water, allowed to partially germinate, and then cured in a kiln by fierce heat. The degree of heat determines the colour of the finished malt, which can be pale, brown, amber, black or chocolate. All beers are made predominantly from pale malt, which has a high level of enzymes. The malt is taken to a brewery, milled and cleaned, and then mixed with pure, hot brewing water in a large vessel called a mash tun. East Anglia and the Scottish Lowlands are major barley-producing regions. As a result of Britain's proximity to the sea, its barleys are known as 'maritime varieties' and are renowned for the quality of the beers produced. There are many varieties of barley grown in Britain but Maris Otter is considered to be the finest malting barley for brewing. During the mashing process, the enzymes in the malt turn starches into sugar. When most of the sugar has been extracted, the sweet liquid, known as 'wort', is pumped to a copper where it is boiled with hops for up to two hours. The boil extracts the resins, acids and tannins from the hops, which add aroma, flavour and bitterness to the beer and also protect the liquid from infection. Different varieties of hops, like grapes in wine-making, impart a wide spectrum of aromas and flavours to beer: spicy, peppery, resiny, floral and citric. At the end of the copper boil, the 'hopped wort' is cooled and is then run into fermenting vessels where yeast is blended in or 'pitched'. Brewer's yeast is carefully cultured and kept refrigerated to avoid contamination from wild yeasts in the air. Strains of yeast vary from brewery to brewery and give their own powerful flavours and characteristics to each beer.

There are two main families of beer: ale and lager. Almost without exception, the beers mentioned in this book are members of the ale family and are produced by a method known as warm fermentation. (In spite of the historic divide between unhopped ale and hopped beer, all ales are brewed with hops today.) Lager brewing, developed in continental Europe during the industrial revolution, involves cold fermentation and the storing of beer at low temperatures. Warm fermentation results in beers with rich, fruity, biscuity aromas and flavours. The British Isles produces an enormous diversity of ales: mild ale, pale ale, bitter, special bitters, porters, stouts, old ales, barley wines and winter warmers.

Mowing

THE MALT

At Tuckers Maltings in Devon a member of staff spreads barley over the heated floor and constantly turns it to aerate it. The covering of grain is known as a 'couch'. Aerating encourages a strong germination that begins to turn starch into sugar inside each ear of barley. If the couch is not turned regularly the sprouting grains will knit together and form a thick and unusable carpet.

West Country

BLUE ANCHOR,
CORNWALL

THE WESTERN END of England, with its strong Celtic traditions in Cornwall, has for centuries been better known for cider than for beer. Both types of drink, essentially rural, have suffered from the hammer blows of rising then falling industrialization. The small armies of miners, shipbuilders and fishermen who needed reviving and refreshing glasses of drink made from barley or apple have either disappeared or find their livelihoods under threat of extinction. A region that survives today mainly on the tourist trade, the West Country puts great pressure on brewers and cider makers when visitors, in the words of a director of the St Austell Brewery, 'fall off the cliffs every September'. Today, in the whole of the West Country, St Austell is the one remaining major commercial country brewery. It has a fine visitor centre that celebrates brewing in Cornwall and a brewhouse packed with magnificent Victorian vessels. Choice and diversity have been revived thanks to the verve and enthusiasm of a clutch of new craft brewers who have set up in farms, cottages, old mills and former breweries to fashion beers with enticing flavours and to recover long-forgotten styles. The West Country is also home to one of England's oldest – possibly the oldest – brewpubs, the Blue Anchor in Helston, which makes its powerful 'stingo' ales on a site where monks brewed centuries earlier.

Visitors to the West Country can not only drink fine ales in some superb and often ancient pubs but can also enjoy the pleasures of a region with sumptuous rural scenery and some historic towns and cities. Cornwall, Devon and Somerset have their wild and solitary moors and tors, still gripped by fearsome legends and mythical beasts, interspersed by handsome towns and charming villages. While this book is fundamentally about beer and breweries, a visit to the West Country offers a chance to sample the products of the small cider makers, much more of an endangered species even than brewers. The rise of a handful of giant cider makers, who produce pale and heavily carbonated drinks aimed at the lager generation, has put great pressure on the makers of true ciders, already savaged by punitive taxes. Seek and sample their wares along with the great ales of the region.

BLACKAWTON

The Blackawton Brewery holds a
hallowed place in the hearts of beer
lovers: it was one of the first of the
breed of new small or 'micro' breweries
that started to improve choice and
diversity after the locust years of the
1960s and 1970s when many larger
breweries had been taken over and
closed down. Blackawton took its name
from the village in which it was founded
in 1977. In its early days, beer was
brewed from malt extract, a syrup
provided for brewers without sufficient
equipment to use malted barley. Today
Blackawton, now in bigger premises
near Totnes, brews in the approved
fashion with mash tuns and coppers,
and the beers are all-malt brews, free
from sugar and additives, although
spices are used in a winter ale.
Blackawton owns no pubs but supplies
some fifty free houses. It is a sad sign of
the times that Blackawton is now the
oldest brewery in Devon.
BEERS: Bitter, Devon Gold, Shepherds
Delight, 44 Special, Nell Gwyn, Winter
Fuel and Headstrong.

BLUE ANCHOR

This wonderfully unspoilt old thatched
inn claims – and there are no known
competitors – to be the oldest brewpub
in Britain. It dates from the year 1400
when it was a monks' resting place. At a
time when water was unsafe to drink,
the inn naturally made ale for the
monks and has continued to brew ever
since. The beers today recall a time
when ale was strong and not taxed to
oblivion. The 'weakest ale' is more than
5 per cent alcohol and there are stories
about a Christmas Special of 11 per
cent that extended the holiday season by
several days for those who imbibed it: it
has now been toned down to a mere 7.6
per cent. The inn has a series of small,
rambling, beamed rooms that are served
by a central corridor. The floors are
flagstoned, tables have been made from
old beer casks and one room has a large,
stone, inglenook fireplace. There is a
skittle alley and customers are usually
welcome to visit both the ancient
brewhouse across the back yard and the
pub cellars where the beers are stored.
BEERS: Middle, Best, Special, Easter
Special, Christmas Special.

BUTCOMBE

Butcombe, based on a former farm, is only a few miles from Bristol but is almost lost down country lanes against a backdrop of the gentle Mendip Hills. It is one of the most successful of the country's small craft breweries, founded in 1978 by Simon Whitmore who had worked in Britain and abroad for several large brewing groups, finishing as Managing Director of Courage Western in Bristol. For years he brewed just one beer, Butcombe Bitter, refusing to follow other craft brewers down the route of producing a vast portfolio of ales. It was a successful strategy, for he has three times doubled the capacity of his spick and span brewhouse, with mashing, boiling and fermenting taking place in converted byres and stalls, and 'racking' (running the finished beer into casks) in former barns. In 1996 Simon Whitmore bowed to demand and added a stronger best bitter. As an experienced brewer, he uses the finest but not the cheapest malting barley, Maris Otter, and a complex range of hops including English Fuggles and Northdown, and German Northern Brewer.

BEERS: Butcombe Bitter, Wilmot's Premium Ale.

COTLEIGH

Cotleigh has come a long way from its humble beginnings in a stable block at Cotleigh Farm in Somerset in 1979. The founders, John and Jennifer Aries, have since moved to specially converted buildings in the old Somerset brewing town of Wiveliscombe, just a few yards from near neighbour and friendly competitor, Exmoor Ales. The spacious brewhouse can produce around 150 barrels of beer a week, sold to some 150 pubs within a forty-mile radius. The Aries have won many awards for the distinctive design of beer labels and pump clips: most of the beers are named after breeds of birds. One of the joys of drinking in Wiveliscombe is to sample Cotleigh beers against those from Exmoor and to marvel at the fact that while both breweries use the same water supply and similar malts and hops, the end products are remarkably dissimilar.

BEERS: Harrier SPA, Tawny Bitter, Barn Owl Bitter, Old Buzzard plus a wide range of occasional and seasonal beers including Goshawk, Peregrine Porter, Golden Eagle, Osprey and Snowy Ale.

COTTAGE

Chris Norman was an airline pilot and keen home-brewer who took early retirement to turn his hobby into a commercial venture, albeit a small one. The name of the company was chosen deliberately to underscore the fact that it is a cottage industry. With his wife Helen, Chris Norman converted the garage at their home at West Lydford in 1993 into a tiny, five-barrel brewery and doubled capacity the following year. In 1995 Cottage, in Chris Norman's words, moved up a notch to become a bungalow business when he won the coveted title of Champion Beer of Britain with Norman's Conquest barley wine. (There is a hidden pun in the title as the starting gravity of the beer is 1066.) The success of Norman's Conquest, available in bottle-fermented as well as draught form, forced the Normans to move to larger premises in an old cheese dairy near Castle Cary, where they have again doubled their output. Most of the beers have a railway theme and are served nationally in around 450 outlets. Local deliveries are made by steam lorry and horse-drawn dray.

BEERS: Southern Bitter, Wheeltappers Ale, Champflower, Golden Arrow, Somerset & Dorset Ale, Our Ken, Great Western Ale and Norman's Conquest.

EXE VALLEY

A brewery in a superb rural setting, based in an old farm barn, Exe Valley started life in 1984 as Barron Brewery, named after founder Richard Barron. The name changed in 1991 when the company expanded and Guy Sheppard joined as a partner. A new plant was installed in 1993 to treble output but the emphasis remains on natural ingredients and quality beers: the brewing water is drawn from the farm's own spring and Pipkin malt is blended with traditional Fuggles, Goldings and Target hops. The main beer, Exe Valley Bitter, is based on an old West Country recipe. Around forty pubs sell the beers within a thirty-mile radius of the brewery.

BEERS: Exe Valley Bitter, Devon Summer, Barron's Hopsit, Dob's Best Friend, Spring Beer, Autumn Glory, Devon Glory, Sheppard's Crook, Exeter Old Bitter and Winter Glow.

EXMOOR

Exmoor began business with a meteoric rise to fame. Founded in 1980 it won the CAMRA Champion Beer of Britain award with one of its first brews of Exmoor Ale and has never looked back since then. It is based in Hancock's Victorian brewery, which ceased production in 1959. The site gave Exmoor the enviable position of being a small craft brewery with proper facilities and space for mash tuns, coppers and fermenters from the beginning, rather than having to convert and expand a barn, a farm building or a lock-up. In addition to the launch pad of the Champion Beer of Britain accolade, Exmoor has won many other awards for its beers, including thirty for Exmoor Gold, one of the first of a new breed of extremely pale bitters created to counter the lager culture of younger drinkers. Brewed only from pale malt, it has ten units of colour, making it only fractionally darker than a genuine Pilsner, while a generous dose of Challenger, Fuggles and Goldings hops gives the beer a superb aroma and palate bursting with hop resins and citric fruit. Exmoor has around 250 outlets in south-west England.

BEERS: Exmoor Ale, Fox, Gold, Hart, Stag, Beast and Exmas.

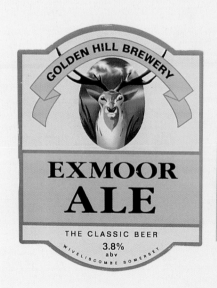

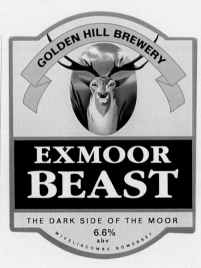

OAKHILL

Oakhill started life in 1984 in the fermentation room of a former brewery of the same name that was founded in 1767 and burnt down in 1924. Oakhill 'Mark II' expanded trade sufficiently to make a move to bigger premises necessary and found them in an old maltings in the town that had once supplied the original brewery. Set high in the Mendip Hills, Oakhill has one of the finest settings in the country and has restored brewing interest in this remote part of Somerset. The beers are complex, rich and fruity and some use imported American Willamette hops that add a profound citrus fruit character. The brewery owns four pubs and serves a further 100 outlets in the region.

BEERS: Somer Ale, Best Bitter, Black Magic, Mendip Gold, Yeoman Strong Ale and Mendip Tickler.

OTTER

Experienced brewer David McCaig swapped his career with Whitbread in Liverpool for an idyllic setting in Devon at the head-spring of the River Otter that both gives its name to his beers and supplies water for the brewery. Otter, launched in 1990, had to survive the disaster of a yeast infection in its early days. It could have been the ruination of many small craft breweries, but David McCaig's expertise enabled him to get a fresh supply of yeast and culture it to avoid any future calamities. This was the springboard for a major expansion with a new brewhouse capable of producing 135 barrels a week. The beers are all-malt, using Halcyon and Maris Otter varieties, with Challenger, Fuggles and Goldings hops. Around ninety pubs in the south-west serve the beers. Bright and Head are also available in bottle form.

BEERS: Bitter, Bright, Ale, Dark and Head.

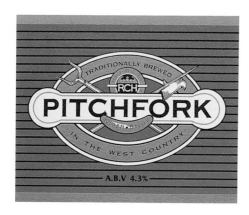

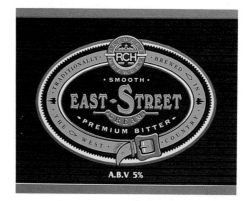

RCH

RCH stood originally for Royal Clarence Hotel as the brewery started life in the 1980s attached to the hotel in Burnham-on-Sea. But increasing demand forced owner Paul Davy and his brewer, Graham Dunbavan, to move to new premises in – fittingly enough in Somerset – an old cider mill near Weston-super-Mare. The former site is recalled in RCH's Old Slug Porter: slugs were a problem in the brewery though they never got into the beer. But the thick collar of foam that the beer creates and the 'lacework' that the foam leaves down the side of the glass reminded Paul Davy of the trails left by the slugs. 1998 was a remarkable year for the brewery. Old Slug Porter beer in bottle-fermented form won a gold medal at the Tuckers Maltings Beer Festival in Newton Abbot, Pitchfork won the Best Bitter class in the Champion Beer of Britain competition and Firebox won a gold medal in 1998 at the Taste of the West Show. Pitchfork takes its name from the 1685 Pitchfork Rebellion in Sedgemoor while Firebox recalls the age of steam railways.

BEERS: Hewish IPA, PG Steam, Pitchfork, Old Slug Porter, East Street Cream, Firebox.

ST AUSTELL

St Austell is the last major commercial brewery in Cornwall, founded in 1851 by maltster and wine merchant Walter Hicks. Hicks was so successful that by 1893 he had to move to bigger premises, where the brewery stands today, built from local stone and, from its high position, dominating the small Cornish town with its imposing façade and tall brewhouse chimney. Inside, the spacious brewhouse has gleaming mash tuns and coppers, and traditional high-sided fermenting vessels. The company is still owned by descendants of Walter Hicks, whose name is commemorated in the premium bitter HSD, which stands for Hicks Special Draught. Superb brewing water is drawn from a nearby aquifer, and pale and coloured malts are balanced by the finest hop varieties of Fuggles and Goldings. The most recent addition to St Austell's portfolio, Trelawny's Pride, recalls a march on London in 1688 by an army of 200,000 Cornishmen demanding the release from the Tower of London of Bishop Trelawny, jailed for seditious libel against James II. St Austell owns 160 pubs and has built a fine visitor centre at the brewery that includes a shop and fascinating brewing artefacts. It opens from Monday to Friday.
BEERS: Bosun's Bitter, XXXX Mild, Dartmoor Best Bitter, Tinners Ale, Trelawny's Pride, HSD and Winter Warmer.

TEIGNWORTHY

John Lawton's small craft brewery has a perfect setting; at one end of Tuckers Victorian maltings in Newton Abbot. He has the pick of the crop of the finest Maris Otter pale malt produced in a highly traditional floor maltings where the grain is turned by hand and encouraged to germinate. The brewery was founded in 1994 and additional vessels have been installed to produce around forty-five barrels of beer a week. John Lawton, who previously brewed with Oakhill and Ringwood, has also added a bottling line to supply a range of bottle-fermented ales for Tuckers' shop. The brewery takes its name from Devon's major river, the Teign, which is pronounced either 'Tin' or 'Tayn' depending on which part of the county you come from. The main beer, Reel Ale, is dedicated to the fishermen who line the banks of the river.

BEERS: Reel Ale, Spring Tide, Beachcomber and Maltster's Ale.

SOUTHERN ENGLAND

BOILING COPPERS,
THOMAS HARDY BREWERY,
DORCHESTER

THE VAST REGION south of London has a rich tradition of beer-making, due in part to the presence in its midst of the great hop fields of Kent. For centuries, brewers in the south had first choice of the hops from Kent, where the plant that gives bitterness and aroma to beer was introduced by Flemish traders in the fifteenth century. The hop industry went into severe decline in the 1970s and 1980s when large national brewing combines turned their back on traditional ale, which needs the robust aromas and flavours of English hops, and concentrated on ersatz lagers with hops imported from the continent. But the revival of traditional ale has encouraged farmers to plant Kentish varieties of hops once more and to impregnate English ales with their spicy and peppery characters. The region has withstood the decline of country brewing better than most other areas. and enjoys the rich, full-bodied and tangy ales from the likes of Arkells, Hall & Woodhouse, Gale's, Harveys, King & Barnes, Palmer, Ushers and Wadworth that stand in magnificent buildings, dating from Georgian as well as Victorian times. The Thomas Hardy Brewery in Dorchester celebrates the bard of Wessex who wrote glowingly about the beers of 'Casterbridge' (Dorchester), 'It was of the most beautiful colour that the eye of an artist in beer could ever desire; full in body, yet brisk as a volcano; piquant, yet without a twang; luminous as an autumn sunset; free from streakiness of taste but finally, rather heady.' Shepherd Neame of Kent celebrated the distinction of being England's oldest brewery, 300 years old in 1998. The beers of these sturdy country brewers have been enriched by the arrival of new, small craft brewers in recent years, based on hop farms, forges and sawmills. Among the craft breweries, Ringwood has pride of place. In 1999 it celebrated twenty-one years of brewing and its survival and startling growth have encouraged others – often keen home-brewers willing to go the extra mile and make beer on a commercial scale – to set up in business. The founder of Ringwood, Peter Austin, has now retired but he is venerated both in Britain and the United States as the father of small craft brewing. With several hundred small breweries in Britain and close to a thousand in the U.S., his contribution to drinkers' pleasure should never be underestimated.

ARCHERS

Archers, as befits a brewery in Swindon, has powerful links with the railways. In 1979, Mark Wallington, a former Royal Air Force officer, opened his small craft brewery under the arches at Swindon railway station, in a former Great Western carriage shed, built at the time when Isambard Kingdom Brunel was building his iron way from London to the West Country. The brewery's first beer, Village Bitter, took its name from the collection of Brunel's Great Western workshops known as 'the Railway Village'. Archers flourished, and Mark Wallington bought three pubs and built up substantial business in some 200 outlets in the area. In 1996 demand finally proved too much for his small, 150-barrels-a-week plant and he moved to a new site based in a former railway engine weighing shed built in 1904. With a brewing chimney and a gabled tower, the building now looks for all the world like a typical turn-of-the-century brewery. The brewing vessels are modern stainless steel but production is based on traditional nineteenth-century 'tower' lines, with brewing water, malt and hops on the top floors feeding mash tuns, coppers and fermenters on floors below. Production has doubled since Archers moved to its new site. There are plans to open a pub in the complex.

BEERS: Village Bitter, Best Bitter, Black Jack Porter, Golden Bitter, Headbanger, plus seasonal beers. Golden Bitter is also available in bottle-fermented form.

ARKELLS

Arkells in an almost rural setting on the edge of Swindon is one of the last of Britain's regional breweries where all the shares are still held by members of the ruling family. The current managing director, James Arkell, is the great-great-grandson of John Arkell who founded the brewery in 1843. In the Victorian manner, a house in the grounds provides accommodation for the head brewer. The brick-built brewery is magnificent, dominated by a tall chimney. In the three-storey main block, hot and cold liquor tanks (brewers always call water 'liquor') and a grain silo feed a malt mill, which grinds the grain, and wood-jacketed mash tuns, where water and grain are blended. The sweet liquid known as wort is pumped to traditional coppers where the whole flowers of Fuggles and Goldings hops are added to the boil. Fermentation is in open square vessels. Visitors to the brewery can enjoy a glass of beer in the brewhouse in a handsome bar area with intriguing brewery artefacts. Arkells' two main beers have the enigmatic names of 2B and 3B, recalling the 19th-century practice of branding wooden casks with simple descriptors when breweries had a large number of products. Arkells owns eighty-six pubs and also supplies some 200 other accounts in the area.

BEERS: 2B, 3B, Kingsdown Ale and seasonal ales Yeomanry, Peter's Porter and Noel Ale.

BALLARD'S

Ballard's began life in 1980 at Cumbers Farm in Trotton and is one of the oldest and most successful of the new breed of micro-brewers. It was launched at a time of economic recession and plummeting beer sales but survived, grew and moved to an industrial estate fashioned from an old sawmill in 1988. Unlike many cramped micros, Ballard's has a comparatively spacious brewhouse with a large mash tun and copper. The driving force behind the brewery is Carola Brown who supplies around sixty outlets in Sussex and Hampshire with her beers. As well as draught ales, she also makes bottle-fermented beers, including an annual ale with a strength to match the year: the 1998 beer was called Blizzard and was 9.8 per cent alcohol. Carola Brown is a passionate advocate for small craft brewers, arguing with the British and European governments that they should enjoy lower rates of duty than bigger breweries. She is the chairwoman of the Society of Independent Brewers.
BEERS: Midhurst Mild, Trotton Bitter, Best Bitter, Wild, Wassail. Wassail is also available in bottle-fermented form.

BUNCE'S

Bunce's is based in a building with a fascinating history. When the War Department bought land on Salisbury Plain in 1898 one building was recorded as 'house, mill, buildings and pasture – two roods, twenty-two perches'. A mill had stood on the site for some 600 years and milling continued until 1911 but little remains of the original building. It was refashioned during the First World War as an electricity generating station for Netheravon airfield, using water power from the River Avon. In spite of its military use, it was rebuilt in a red-brick style with a pagoda and loading bay that give it the air of a country maltings. The building then fell into disuse after its sale by the Ministry of Defence in 1983 but was rescued by Tony Bunce who turned it into a small brewery complete with living accommodation in rooms beneath imposing roof trusses. The mill room was converted into a brewhouse with stainless steel mash tuns, coppers and fermenters. In 1993 Danish master brewer Stig Anker Andersen bought the brewery and energetically expanded the beer range. In spite of his origins, he concentrates on traditional warm-fermented English ales, although he adds sweet gale, an old Viking brewing ingredient, to his autumn beer Stig Swig.
BEERS: Benchmark, Pigswill, Second to None, Danish Dynamite, Old Smokey, Stig Swig plus seasonal brews.

CHERITON

The Cheriton Brewhouse was built in 1993 to supply the Flower Pots Inn on the same site. The purpose-built, ten-barrel brewery is in a functional building like a large garage but the pub is a delightful rural retreat with two small bars decked out with old country tools, open fires and traditional pub games. You can enjoy the beers on the front and back lawns where morris dancers occasionally perform in summer. Brewery and pub are close to the site of one of the final battles of the English Civil War. The pub once belonged to the retired head gardener of nearby Avington Park who gave it its unusual name. The Mid-Hants Steam Railway – the Watercress Line – starts close by at Alresford, and Cheriton beers are sometimes available on the trains. The brewery also owns a second pub and supplies some forty other outlets in the area. Three of the beers have won major prizes in their categories in the annual Champion Beer of Britain competition.

BEERS: Pots Ale, Best Bitter, Diggers Gold, Flower Power plus seasonal brews.

DONNINGTON

The Cotswolds, the captivating area of Gloucestershire full of small towns and villages of mellow stone buildings, has the most idyllic setting for a brewery in England. Donnington, down a narrow road near Stow-on-the-Wold, is fronted by a mill pond where geese, swans and weeping willow trees provide an exquisite backdrop. The water turns a wheel of a mill that provides all the power for the small brewhouse. The mill was once part of a feudal estate that dates from 1291. In the sixteenth century it was used as a cloth mill and was converted to grind corn around 1580. It became a bakehouse until the Arkell family from Swindon bought the mill and the surrounding buildings in 1827 and Richard Arkell started to brew there in 1865. His grandson Claude still brews in Swindon, and carries on the tradition of making hand-crafted country beers. His brewing water comes from a spring beside the mill pond while his Fuggles hops are from neighbouring Worcestershire. Local barley was used until the 1960s but Mr Arkell now buys the finest Maris Otter variety from Norfolk. His bitters are rich and rounded, dominated by a spicy Fuggles bitterness and complemented by biscuity malt. Donnington owns fifteen pubs within striking distance of the brewery, several offering accommodation as well as fine ales and simple rustic food.

BEERS: XXX Mild, BB and SBA.

GALE'S

George Gale is Hampshire's major brewery. Founded in 1847 on the London Road in Horndean, an important coach route from the capital to Portsmouth, the brewery first stood on the site of the Ship and Bell Hotel, which is now the 'brewery tap', where the first casks of a new brew are always available. The first brewery was destroyed by fire and a new plant was built alongside in 1869 and extended in 1983. The brick buildings, dominated by an imposing tower, have some splendid old vessels inside, including round wooden fermenters bound by metal hoops, and fine traditional mash tuns and coppers. As well as having to be rebuilt after a fire, other disasters include the loss of a head brewer who committed suicide by falling into a vat of his fermenting beer. The company is still family owned, has 122 pubs and supplies 550 other outlets. To mark the 150th anniversary in 1997, an old malt store was turned into a reception area with a bar, decorated by many fascinating old photographs and prints of the brewery and the brewing process. As well as its distinctive draught beers, Gale's also produces a renowned bottle-fermented beer, Prize Old Ale, in hand-corked bottles, which improves for many years and develops an apple-like fruitiness. The brewery's Butser Bitter is named after a local hill, the Butser.
BEERS: Butser Bitter, GB, Winter Brew, HSB and Festival Mild, plus seasonal brews and Prize Old Ale in bottle.

HALL & WOODHOUSE

A famous Dorset brewery that is better known by its symbol of the badger, so much so that it now trades as the Badger Brewery. The company dates from 1777 when a farmer, Charles Hall, founded a brewery in Ansty and made his fortune by supplying ale to troops in Weymouth who were preparing to fight the French. In 1847 the Halls joined forces with the Woodhouse family, who also lived in Ansty: their former house is now a Hall & Woodhouse pub, the Fox. A new brewery was built in the 1890s in the elegant Georgian town of Blandford Forum, which was rebuilt to its present design after most of the town was destroyed in a fire in 1731. Some of the original houses remain, their darker brick work balancing the pale stone of the Georgian buildings. The brewery, on the edge of the town, alongside the River Star and overlooking fields, is a fine example of Victorian architecture. It was built by John Wells and Sons in 1899 at a cost of £28,000 and took just fifteen months to complete. It was bought by Hall & Woodhouse at the turn of the century. The brewhouse is fiercely traditional: the wooden mash tuns have copper lids, the boiling coppers are vast and dome-shaped, and the fermenting vessels have high wooden sides to contain the vast yeast head.
BEERS: IPA, Dorset Best and Tanglefoot.

THOMAS HARDY

This magnificent red-brick complex is one of the finest examples of Victorian brewery architecture, dominated by a soaring chimney and sloping brewhouse tower. The company was founded as the Green Dragon Brewery by the Eldridge family in 1837 who later joined forces with the Pope family. For most of its life the brewing concern was known as Eldridge Pope but was renamed Thomas Hardy in 1996. The Wessex writer and poet wrote glowingly about the ales from Dorchester, the town he called Casterbridge in his novels. In 1968 the brewery produced a bottled beer for a Hardy festival as a one-off product which proved so popular that it became a regular beer. Thomas Hardy's Ale, 12 per cent alcohol, is bottle-fermented and will improve if laid down for at least twenty-five years. Along with the other beers, Thomas Hardy's Ale is produced in a superb brewhouse with cast-iron mash tuns, great domed boiling coppers shaped like deep-sea diving bells, and high-sided wooden fermenters to which side boards are added to keep the great bubbling head of yeast in place.
BEERS: Pope's Traditional Bitter, Hardy Country Bitter, Royal Oak and Thomas Hardy's Ale.

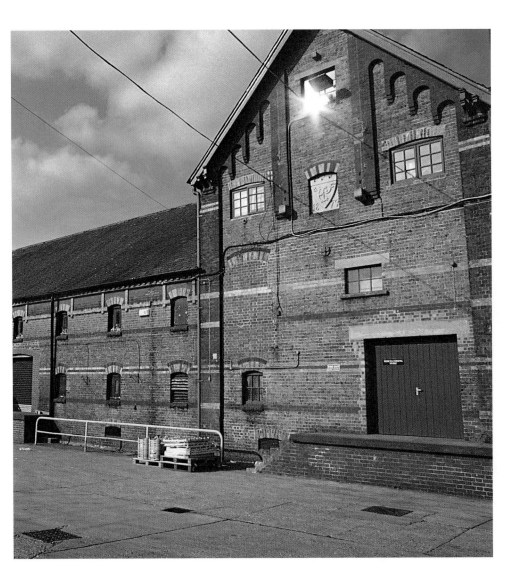

HARVEYS

Harveys' Georgian brewery stands in a commanding position alongside the River Ouse. It was built in the late eighteenth century by John Harvey and rebuilt in 1881. The Victorian Gothic tower is a classic of the style and has replicas at Hook Norton in Oxfordshire and Tolly Cobbold in Ipswich. The red-brick building has some delightful tall, arched windows in black and white timber frames. At the far end of the brewhouse, a tall, thickset, hooped chimney is built of paler brick. The brewing process flows simply and logically from floor to floor to avoid the use of pumps. From the top, a malt mill feeds the mash tuns, coppers and fermenters on the floors below. Turn-of-the-century steam-driven vehicles are on show at the brewery that boasts close links with Tom Paine, who was an excise officer in Lewes before achieving greater fame as the author of *The Rights of Man* and an influential figure in both the American and French revolutions. Harveys, still family owned, brews a Tom Paine seasonal ale in his memory every year.
BEERS: Sussex XX Mild Ale, Sussex Pale Ale, Sussex Best Bitter, Sussex XXXX Old Ale, Armada Ale, plus seasonal ales and a bottle-fermented Porter.

HOGS BACK

Hogs Back takes its name from the long, narrow ridge that is one of the features of the surrounding Surrey countryside. The brewery was established in 1992 in old farm buildings that date from around 1768 and there is now a modern brewhouse inside the charming and bucolic façade. New equipment was installed in 1997 to double capacity and from just one beer in 1992 – TEA, which stands for Traditional English Ale – Hogs Back now produces twenty or more beers on a regular, seasonal or occasional basis. Pipkin pale malt and Fuggles and Goldings English hops are the basis of all the beers. The head brewer is a woman – a brewster – and Brewster's Bundle was named in her honour when she had a child.

BEERS: Dark Mild, APB, TEA, Blackwater Porter, Hop Garden Gold, RIP Snorter, YES, Fuggles Nouveau, Utopia, OTT, Brewster's Bundle, Santa's Wobble and A Over T. TEA, Brewster's Bundle and A Over T are also available in bottle-fermented form along with a 7.5 per cent ale called Wobble in a Bottle.

KING & BARNES

The King family has been brewing in Horsham since 1800 and moved to its present site in 1850. It merged with Barnes' brewery in 1906 at a time of great turbulence in the brewing industry. A parliamentary Beer Act of 1830, introduced by free marketeers with the aim of weakening the power of the brewers, had allowed any citizen to open a small pub on payment of one guinea. The Act was a disaster. Apart from wide-scale drunkenness among the populace, most of the owners of the new licensed premises (known as 'Tom and Jerry houses') quickly went bust. The brewers rushed to buy up the bankrupt stock but many overstretched themselves financially and staved off disaster by merging with local rivals. A powerful temperance movement at the turn of the century also encouraged further mergers. Since 1906 King & Barnes has seen off wars and depressions to become one of the most successful of the country's independent family brewers, still run by the Kings. A new stainless steel brewhouse was installed in 1980 but the old brewhouse, housing a circular mash tun with a slatted wooden jacket, and a copper boiling kettle, is still in use for short-run beers. As well as producing a fine range of cask-conditioned ales, King & Barnes has pioneered the revival of bottle-fermented beers.

BEERS: Mild Ale, Sussex, Broadwood, Old Ale, and Festive plus seasonal and bottle-fermented ales.

LARKINS

Larkins Brewery is situated on a hop farm in Kent, the ideal base for brewing ales with powerful and tempting aromas of resins, peppers and spices. The brewery takes its name from the farm but is owned by the Dockerty family who started brewing in 1986 when they bought the Royal Tunbridge Wells Brewery. They moved to Larkins Farm in 1989 and converted an old barn to contain the brewing equipment. An additional boiling copper and fermenters were added in 1991 to cope with demand. The beers, which are all-malt and additive-free, are available in around sixty pubs in the south-east and are brewed from Kentish hop varieties, including some grown on Larkins Farm, where they are dried and stored in a traditional oast house. The hops used are Fuggles, Whitbread Goldings Variety and the prized East Kent Golding: like grapes, hops will only grow in the right soil and East Kent produces the finest Goldings. (An area of Kent that has poor soil for hop growing is known as 'bastard Kent'.) Among the cask-conditioned ales, the Porter is acclaimed as one of the finest of the style with its deep chocolate malt and bitter hops character.
BEERS: Traditional Ale, Chiddingstone Bitter, Best Bitter and Porter.

MOLE'S

Roger Catté, a former brewer with Ushers of Trowbridge (where his nickname was Mole), started his own business in 1982 and runs a traditional brewhouse that produces cask-conditioned ales for sixteen pubs owned by the company and a further 100 free trade outlets. The basis of the beers is Maris Otter barley malt with Fuggles, Whitbread Goldings Variety and Bramling Cross hop varieties.
BEERS: Tap Bitter, Best Bitter, Barley Mole, Landlords Choice and Brew 97. Brew 97 is also available in bottle-fermented form.

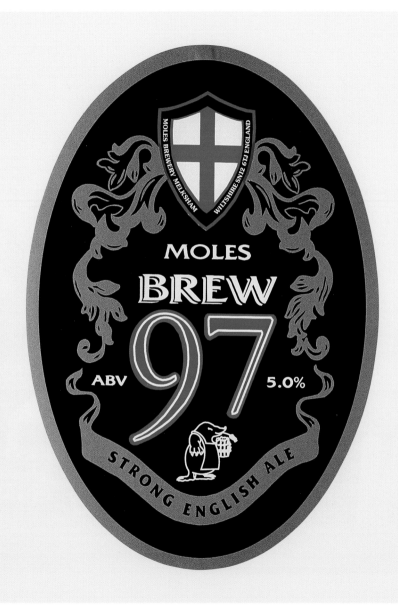

OLD FORGE

Village blacksmiths, by repute, were prodigious drinkers of ale, cooling their sweating brows and restoring lost energy with frequent tankards. The owners of Old Forge reinforced the bucolic image by setting up their brewery in a restored village forge in 1995. Confusingly, the company is called Pett Brewing but trades under the Old Forge name. Fifty pubs supply the beers, and the Priory in Hastings uses the Old Forge sign and always has at least two of the beers on sale.
BEERS: Brothers Best, Pett Progress, Pett Genius, Summer Eclipse and Ewe Could Be So Lucky.

PALMER'S

Palmer's brewery is set in beautiful mellow stone buildings close to the sea and the chalk cliffs of Dorset. One building is thatched and at the rear of the brewhouse a large waterwheel stands alongside a river, though the wheel is now purely decorative and no longer supplies power. The brewery is ancient, founded in 1794 in a former mill and bought by the Palmer brothers, John Cleeves and Robert Henry, a century later. A further century on, the company is still run by two Palmer brothers, one of whom is called Cleeves. The brewery is spacious and elegant, the beer made in fine traditional vessels. English pale and crystal malts are blended with hops from England, the U.S. and Slovenia, including Mount Hood from the Pacific North-west and Styrian Goldings from Slovenia. Palmer's Bridport Bitter at just 3.2 per cent is one of the last of a south-west England style known as 'boy's bitters'; low in alcohol but bursting with rich hop flavours, developed to refresh agricultural workers. Such beers were the rural equivalent of the mild ales of industrial cities. A beer called 200 was brewed to mark the brewery's two hundred years of activity and is now a permanent product.
BEERS: Bridport Bitter, Best Bitter or IPA, Tally Ho! and 200.

POOLE

Poole Brewery was opened by David Rawlins in 1980 and he moved the plant ten years later to his one and only pub, the Brewhouse. Additional fermenting vessels were installed in the mid-1990s and Poole can now produce some seventy-five barrels a week. The brewery's logo is a dolphin, occasionally seen in the great sweep of Poole Harbour. Visitors can travel by boat to Brownsea Island, home to one of the last surviving groups of red squirrels in Britain. Lord Baden Powell used the island to launch the Boy Scout movement.

BEERS: Dolphin Best Bitter, Bedrock Bitter, Holes Bay Hog, Bosun Bitter and Double Barrel.

QUAY

Quay has brought brewing back to Weymouth ten years after the seaside resort and harbour town lost its Devenish brewery. Devenish, which also had a plant in Cornwall, stopped brewing when new owners decided to concentrate on pub retailing, using nationally-promoted beers from bigger breweries. The large Victorian Weymouth brewery is now owned and run as a leisure outlet by the Warrington-based pub group Greenalls but Quay is independent and is part of the Timewalk theme that allows visitors to immerse themselves in nineteenth-century industry and nostalgia. Quay's beers are on sale in the Victorian Tastings Bar and shop. One draught ale, Weymouth JD 1742, is named in honour of John Devenish, founder of the old brewery company. Regular beers are topped up with seasonal ones and bottle-fermented beers.

BEERS: Weymouth Special Ale, Weymouth JD 1742, Bombshell Bitter and Old Rott, plus seasonal and bottle-fermented ales.

RECTORY

It sounds like the plot of a TV soap opera, but in real life the Rector of Plumpton, Godfrey Broster, started a small brewery in 1996 to bring in finance for the maintenance of the three churches in his parish. His parishioners raised the money to buy the brewing equipment and a further injection of capital enabled production to be doubled. The rector moved to his present, larger premises on a farm in 1997 and he now supplies a dozen local pubs. In the autumn of 1998 Godfrey Broster signed up as a 'pupil' or apprentice at Harveys of Lewes to improve his brewing skills.
BEERS: Rector's Pleasure, Parson's Porter, Light Relief, Rector's Revenge and Christmas Cheer.

RINGWOOD

Ringwood has a special place in the micro-brewery revolution of the past twenty-five years. It was not only one of the first of the breed but its success encouraged others to invest in small brewing plants and help restore choice and diversity to drinkers and pubs. Ringwood was founded by Peter Austin, now honoured in Britain and the U.S.A. as the grandfather of micro-brewing. He came out of retirement to brew again and as well as Ringwood has helped set up small breweries in many countries, including the U.S.A., France, China and Africa. Launched in 1978, the brewery moved to attractive new premises in part of the former Tunks brewery. To meet demand for the beers, a new brewhouse was commissioned in 1994 and a new fermenting room was added a year later. Peter Austin has retired for a second time and the company is now run by David Welsh, who supplies 350 pubs as well as Ringwood's two tied outlets. The brewery's Old Thumper strong ale is a past winner of the Champion Beer of Britain competition and is now brewed under licence in the U.S.A. by Shipyard Brewing in Portland, Maine, which is run by British-born Alan Pugsley who served his apprenticeship at Ringwood.
BEERS: Best Bitter, True Glory, Fortyniner, XXXX Porter and Old Thumper. Fortyniner is also available bottle-fermented.

SHEPHERD NEAME

Shepherd Neame is Britain's oldest brewery. It celebrated 300 years of continuous brewing in 1998. The Faversham Brewery was founded by Captain Richard Marsh, passed into the hands of Samuel Shepherd, a maltster, who was later joined by a hop-farming family, the Neames. The Neames still run the brewery today and while they have carefully developed their business to include lagers, with such brands as the leading Indian lager Kingfisher and the Swiss beer Hürlimann, ales are the bedrock of the company, fashioned in superb old vessels, including teak mash tuns that date from 1910. Old steam engines are still on site and can be brought into use should the electricity supply fail. A restored medieval hall is used as a visitor centre. Shepherd Neame – known simply as 'Sheps' to its devotees – owns 390 pubs and supplies a further 500 outlets. It has been at the forefront of the bottle-fermented beer revival and its Porter is based on an eighteenth-century recipe that included Spanish liquorice. Importantly, being based in the heart of the Kent hop fields, Shepherd Neame has the first pick of the annual Goldings and Target varieties. The importance of hops to the brewery is stressed by a frieze of hops around the entrance to the offices.
BEERS: Master Brew Bitter, Best Bitter, Spitfire Premium Ale, Bishops Finger and Original Porter. Bishops Finger (named after an old Kentish road sign) is also available bottle-fermented.

TISBURY

A Wiltshire brewery with a turbulent history, Tisbury is based in an old village workhouse that was converted into a brewery in 1868 by a local maltster named Archibald Beckett. The site was rebuilt after it was gutted by fire in 1885. Under Beckett's control, the brewery thrived and was one of the first to use steam-driven engines. The company was bought by the eccentric F. H. S. Styring who used his pet monkey as the brewery's official beer taster until the unfortunate creature fell into a vat and was drowned. In spite of the loss of the monkey, the brewery expanded, with deliveries made by horse-drawn drays throughout the Wardour and Nadder valleys and beyond. The brewery stopped production at the outbreak of the First World War and beer did not flow again until 1980 when a new Tisbury Brewery opened on the site. It was replaced by the Wiltshire Brewery which closed down in 1992. Yet another Tisbury Brewery opened three years later with brewing carried out by John Featherby who has also brewed in Andover and Corfu. Tisbury supplies some fifty outlets and uses the slogan 'The small brewery with the big name'. Not surprisingly, the brewery is said to be haunted; whether by a human or a monkey is not known.
BEERS: Best Bitter, Austin Ale, Archibald Beckett, Nadderjack Ale and Old Wardour.

USHERS

Ushers, founded in 1824, is based in superb Georgian buildings in the equally elegant town of Trowbridge. It was once a major brewing force in the region but lost its identity and its reputation for good ale when it was taken over by Watney (later Grand Metropolitan) in 1960. When 'Grand Met' decided to leave brewing, it sold Ushers to Courage who in turn sold the brewery and more than 400 pubs to the Trowbridge management in 1991. Behind the Georgian façade there is now a high-tech modern and multi-functional brewhouse that enables Ushers to brew a wide variety of ales and lagers. The ales are brewed predominantly from Halcyon malts and Target and Styrian Goldings hops but wheat is added to the summer beer while Autumn Frenzy includes a generous addition of malted rye. £6 million has been invested in the brewhouse to enable Ushers to supply a tied estate that has grown to 541 as well as many free trade accounts. As well as seasonal beers and international lagers, Ushers inherited from Watney the old Cockney beer, Manns Brown Ale, which it still brews for a large and appreciative London market.

BEERS: Best Bitter, Spring Fever, Summer Madness, Autumn Frenzy, Founders Ale.

WADWORTH

Wadworth is a champion of tradition. The red-brick Victorian brewery in Devizes still delivers beer to local pubs by horse-drawn drays, while its best-known beer, 6X, recalls the medieval time when monks brewed strong ale and blessed each cask by branding it with Xs to indicate both strength and a blessing from God. Wadworth is one of the few breweries to employ a cooper to make and repair wooden casks. But despite a highly traditional brewhouse, Wadworth, founded by Henry Wadworth in 1885, doesn't live in the past. It has busily expanded its business, brewing around 2,000 barrels of beer a week to supply its 225 pubs and a large number of free trade accounts. 6X has become a national brand thanks to a trading arrangement with Whitbread. The beers are brewed with Pipkin and Halcyon malts and Fuggles and Goldings whole flower hops. An annual harvest ale, Malt and Hops, uses freshly harvested barley malt while Goldings hops are picked the day before brewing and dried overnight.

BEERS: Henry Wadworth, Original IPA, 6X, SummerSault, Farmers Glory and Old Timer plus several seasonal beers.

Thames Valley

Morland brewery,
Oxfordshire

The great tributary of the Thames has had a long association with brewing. Before the arrival of the railway and modern roads, the river transported malt and hops to breweries and finished beer back from them. The importance of the river can be measured by the number of breweries, including such famous London firms as Thrale's Anchor Brewery and John Courage's Brewery, that were built on its banks. The decline of London as an important brewing centre has left just one major riverside brewery, Brakspear, in the delightful regatta town of Henley-on-Thames, commemorated in the poem 'At an Inn in Henley' by William Shenstone, 'Who'er has travell'd life's dull round/Where'er his stages may have been/May sigh to think he still has found/The warmest welcome at an inn' – lines much admired by that celebrated toper, Dr Samuel Johnson. The region is fortunate in being close to both the hop fields of Kent and the barley fields of East Anglia, allowing brewers the pick of the harvest and enabling their beers to develop deep biscuity malt and resiny hop characters. The Thames Valley includes the classic 'tower brewery' of Hook Norton, a utilitarian Victorian design in which the brewing process flows down from floor to floor by gravity, removing the need for pumps. Several new craft breweries have added to the pleasures of beer drinking, including Old Luxters, which makes wine as well as ale and disproves the old adage that the grape and the grain make bad bedfellows. The region is rich in history. Oxford is not only a world-famous seat of learning but has also taken on a more plebeian celebrity due to the bibulous exploits of Chief Inspector Morse in and around the town, solving murders most foul with the aid of copious draughts of ale consumed in delightful country pubs. Close by, the charming town of Woodstock is near to Blenheim Palace, seat of the Marlboroughs and birthplace of Winston Churchill, a politician who achieved rightful popularity by announcing that the armed forces in World War Two should have regular supplies of good beer: he even sanctioned a floating brewery for the Navy. A politician of a different colour, the utopian socialist, artist and designer William Morris, made his home at Kelmscott Manor. Berkshire and Buckinghamshire were much fought over during the English Civil War and the two counties are especially rich in fine rural ale houses where you can sup the products of the breweries in this section.

BRAKSPEAR

Brakspear is one of England's oldest and most revered breweries. Brewing has been taking place at the site since at least 1700. The Brakspear family, which is distantly related to England's only Pope, Nicholas Breakspear, arrived on the brewing scene in 1799 when Robert Brakspear went into partnership with Richard Hayward to run the brewery. It was Robert's son, William Henry, who gave his name to the company. He expanded the enterprise with great enthusiasm, buying pubs in the Thames Valley and even selling his ales in London: boats would take beer to the capital along the Thames and return laden with malt and hops. The brewery and offices are dominated by a magnificent chimney and arched entrance. The brewhouse has fine mash tuns and coppers but the most interesting feature is the rare 'dropping system' of fermentation. Two banks of open-topped fermenting vessels are ranged above each other on two storeys. Fermentation begins in the top vessels and after a few days the bottoms of the vats are opened, and liquid and yeast drop down to the vessels below. The method aerates the yeast and leaves behind dead yeast cells. Fermentation continues with great vigour for several more days.

BEERS: XXX Mild, Bitter, Regatta Gold, Dark Rose, Hop Demon, XXXX Old Ale, Special, Bee Sting, OBJ and Reapers Reward plus an annual bottle-fermented Vintage Ale.

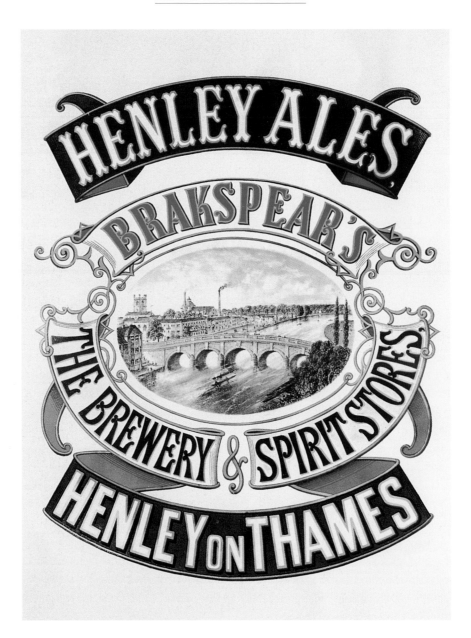

CHILTERN

The Chiltern Brewery is one of the oldest-surviving 'new wave' craft breweries in Britain, set up in 1980 on a small farm near Aylesbury. But Chiltern is far more than just a brewery; it has a shop that specializes in a range of beer-related products including beer mustards, old ale chutneys, beer cheese, liqueur chocolates, and even a hop cologne. There is a small but fascinating museum of brewing in the area and visitors can even stay at the site in self-catering accommodation in a converted barn. The beers are brewed with the finest traditional ingredients: Maris Otter malt, and Challenger, Fuggles and Goldings whole flower hops. One ale, John Hampden's, was brewed in honour of the Member of Parliament for Buckingham and a leading figure in the English Civil War: its first brew was mashed by a direct descendant, the Earl of Buckinghamshire.

BEERS: Chiltern Ale, Beechwood Bitter, Three Hundreds Old Ale (draught and bottle-fermented), John Hampden's and Bodgers Barley Wine (draught and bottle-fermented).

HOOK NORTON

Hook Norton is the name of both brewery and village, the former looming over the small community of cottages and pubs. The brewery is one of the finest in England and is a splendid example of a Victorian 'tower brewery'. It was designed by William Bradford, who also drew up the plans for Harvey's of Lewes and Tolly Cobbold of Ipswich, each bearing his signature of a pagoda tower. Within the brewery, each stage of the production process flows logically down from the floor above by gravity, removing the need for pumps. Hook Norton was built in 1850 by John Harris on the site of a farm maltings and the company is still controlled by his family. Much of the original brewing plant and machinery is still in use, including a 25-horsepower steam engine that draws Cotswold well water to the surface for the mash. The beers, brewed with Maris Otter malts and Challenger, Fuggles and Goldings whole flower hops, have superb biscuity malt and tangy hop character, on sale in thirty-seven delightful country pubs. The celebrated Best Bitter and Old Hooky premium ale have been joined by some new beers, including a wonderfully roasty and chocolaty stout based on a nineteenth-century recipe.
BEERS: Best Mild, Best Bitter, Generation, Old Hooky, Double Stout, Haymaker and Twelve Days.

MORLAND

Morland dates from 1711 and is the second-oldest independent brewery in Britain. It has been on its present site since 1861 and the imposing Victorian grandeur of the buildings includes a splendid brewhouse and fermenting room with traditional round mash tuns, copper boiling kettles and open fermenting 'squares'. In the late 1990s Morland added a second brewhouse to double capacity, based on the success of its national draught and bottled ale, Old Speckled Hen. The curious name is taken from a prototype MG motor car built in Abingdon: the bodywork had a distinctive mottled paint effect that gave it the nickname of the Old Speckled Hen. Although the car never went into production, the prototype could be seen around the town for many years. Morland has a large estate of pubs, many in delightful settings in the Thames Valley. The company achieved some notoriety by buying the celebrated real ale brewery, Ruddles of Rutland, in 1997, transferring the beers to Abingdon and closing the Ruddles plant the following year.
BEERS: Independent IPA, Ruddles Best Bitter, Original Bitter, The Tanners Jack, Ruddles County and Old Speckled Hen.

MORRELLS

Centuries of proud brewing tradition that served town and gown in Oxford were cruelly and crudely snuffed out in the autumn of 1998 when Morrells Brewery closed. It stays in this book because of the splendour of its brewhouse and gilded entrance, and as a reminder that this country's architectural and industrial treasures need to be guarded and protected from those who seek to make a quick profit from asset-stripping. Oxford once had several breweries but Morrells was the oldest and was managed by the family of that name who bought it in 1782. As well as the imposing façade, the brewhouse had some fine old mash tuns, coppers and fermenters, producing full-bodied and rich tasting ales for a substantial pub estate in the Thames Valley. New directors from outside the family ousted chief executive Charles Eld, a Morrell on the distaff side, in the spring of 1998 and his mother, Margie, resigned as a director a few weeks later, declaring that the rest of the board was determined to close the brewery and sell the pubs. She was right. In the autumn of 1998 the company was sold and the new owner said that he saw no future for the brewery. The beers will be brewed under contract for the pubs but as they will no longer be true Morrells' ales they are not listed here.

OLD LUXTERS

They mix both the grape and the grain at Old Luxters, which started in life as a vineyard and winery before branching out into brewing as well. The remote Old Luxters Farm, high in the Chiltern Hills above the village of Hambleden and near Henley-on-Thames, used to be a mixed arable and pig farm. David Ealand bought the site in order to plant vines and make some notable English wines there. A brewery was added in 1990 and is one of the finest and certainly the most handsome of small craft plants with wood-clad mash tun, copper and fermenters. It is located at one end of a vaulted and beamed barn that has won awards for its conversion. Dinners, operas, and wine and beer tastings are hosted there. The brewery uses the finest English malts, and Fuggles and Goldings hops for its range of cask-conditioned and bottle-fermented ales. The brewery planned to add two new bottle-fermented ales in 1999, a pale and refreshing Luxters Gold and a strong Luxters Legend that can be stored for ageing.
BEERS: Barn Ale Bitter, Barn Ale Special and Dark Roast available cask conditioned and bottle-fermented.

WYCHWOOD

Wychwood has been so successful since its launch as the Glenny Brewery in 1983 that it has moved from the ranks of micro-brewery to 'small regional'. It started life in the former maltings of the defunct Clinch's Brewery in Witney. It moved to a new site in 1987 but returned to Clinch's in 1994, developing other parts of the brewery in order to install new equipment to keep up with demand. Wychwood now produces around 500 barrels a week for its thirty Hobgoblin pubs and seventy other outlets. It also produces a large amount of packaged beers for Tesco and other supermarkets. Hobgoblin is now one of the top bottled beers on sale in Britain, a remarkable achievement for a small brewery. An important element of its success is the eye-grabbing nature of its labels and pump clips that depict goblins, witches and other woodland demons and faeries. The notably fruity and full-bodied beers are made with Maris Otter malt and Challenger, Progress, Styrian Goldings and Target hops. Wheat, amber and black malts are added to some beers for colour and flavour.
BEERS: Shires XXX, Fiddlers Elbow, Special, Old Devil, The Dog's Bollocks and Hobgoblin.

Eastern England

GREENE KING,
SUFFOLK

EAST ANGLIA, encompassing Norfolk, Suffolk and parts of Cambridgeshire, is the grain basket of England. The rich alluvial soil, much of it reclaimed from the encroaching North Sea, provides the finest malting barley for the brewing industry. Beers from eastern England have a tradition of being rich in biscuity malt flavours, balanced by generous hop bitterness. The region is equally rich in fine brewing buildings: Adnams' seaside site in Southwold, overlooked by an inshore, whitewashed lighthouse and surrounded by some delightful pubs; Tolly Cobbold by the River Orwell, one of the oldest breweries in England; Elgood's splendid Georgian plant and gardens on the edge of the Fens; Greene King's between-the-wars design with Art Deco touches, blending with the Georgian finery of Bury St Edmunds; and the pleasing Victorian bulk of McMullen's in the old county town of Hertford. One of the most fascinating breweries in the area is also one of the newest, St Peter's, a small craft brewery set in the grounds of a medieval house which also houses religious artefacts.

The region is rich in history. Oliver Cromwell came from Huntingdonshire, killed a king, set up a republic, has a statue outside Parliament but has lost his county to Cambridgeshire. Earlier, Hereward the Wake used the Fens as cover for his daring exploits against the Normans in and around Ely, and came close to defeating them. Colchester is England's oldest town and stands on the site of Camulodunum, a Roman garrison sacked by Boudicca, queen of the Iceni. Norwich is steeped in history and fine buildings though it lost all its breweries thanks to the scorched earth policy of Watney's in the 1970s and Eighties. Cambridge's university was founded in 1284 by the Bishop of Ely, and today has a fascinating clash and complement of buildings, from the timber-framed lodge at Queens' College to the brick and stone grandeur of Trinity.

ADNAMS

Adnams is based in the Suffolk Regency seaside resort of Southwold with its inshore lighthouse that sweeps across the North Sea at night. The brewery was founded in 1890 and grew out of a small beer-making concern on the site of what is now the Swan Hotel. The local Adnamses were joined by the Anglo-Irish Loftus family at the turn of the century: the current chairman is Simon Loftus who also built up the celebrated wine merchant side of the business. The brewery, opposite the Sole Bay Inn and the lighthouse, has been carefully extended, with one section in a row of fishermen's cottages. The brewhouse is magnificent, with fine old mash tuns, coppers and high-sided wooden fermenters. There is no skimping on ingredients: head brewer Mike Powell-Evans uses only the finest Maris Otter malting barley from the East Anglian grain basket, and Fuggles and Goldings whole flower hops. Adnams has won many awards for its beers, including the title of Champion Beer of Britain in 1993 for Extra. Adnams used to draw its brewing water from a well under the sea and although this is no longer used, the beers do have a characteristic hint of salt and seaweed. BEERS: Mild, Bitter, Old Ale, Extra, and Broadside with seasonal ales Regatta (Summer), Oyster Stout (October) and Tally Ho (Christmas).

BATEMANS

Breweries don't come much lovelier than Batemans. Its ivy-covered windmill stands proud across the flatlands of Lincolnshire near Skegness, guarding the entrance to a splendid brewhouse packed with traditional vessels. The company was founded in 1874 by a farmer who was the grandfather of the present chairman, George Bateman. It is not just a family-owned business but one with real roots in the local community. During the economic depression between the two world wars, George Bateman's father had to lay off some workers, then saw them standing around on street corners in Wainfleet and immediately hired them again. The rural charm and family feel of the company was ruptured in the mid-1980s when some of the Batemans decided to sell their shares and retire to the Channel Islands on the proceeds. George Bateman, with the active support of his wife, daughter and son, stumped the country to find the finance to buy out his relations and secure the future of the brewery. Since then Batemans has gone from strength to strength, winning the Champion Beer of Britain competition with its XXXB premium bitter and a clutch of other awards. BEERS: Dark Mild, XB, Hill Billy Bitter, Valiant, Salem Porter, XXXB and Victory Ale plus seasonal and occasional ales called Jolly Jaunts and Mystic Brews.

BLUE MOON

Peter Turner worked in the pub trade
for twenty years then decided to stop
serving other people's beers and make
his own. He opened his tiny brewery on
his farm in January 1997 and has built
the business to the level of 200 gallons
a week for fifty local pubs. He also
offers 'bed and brewer' accommodation
at the farm, which includes a tour of the
brewery. At the end of 1998 Blue
Moon stopped brewing temporarily
while new premises were being sought.
At preseent the beers are being brewed
for Peter Turner by Buffy's (opposite).
BEERS: Easy Life, Dark Side, Sea of
Tranquility, Hingham High, Milk of
Amnesia and Liquor Mortis.

BUFFY'S

There are many breweries attached to
pubs but one standing alongside a
fifteenth-century house is rare
(although not unique: see St Peter's).
Buffy's began life as Mardle Hall
Brewery in 1993 with brewing
equipment bought from Harviestoun in
Scotland. It was forced to change its
name after a complaint from a brewery
with a similar name. Despite that small
set-back, Buffy's has gone from strength
to strength. Owners Roger Abrahams
and Julie Savory installed a new
brewhouse to double their ouput and
now produce thirty barrels of beer a
week for forty local free houses. Roger
and Julie welcome visitors, encourage
them to watch the brewing process –
'Good Norfolk barley, simply malted,
simply mashed with pure and simple
Norfolk water: some say it's simply the
use of good, old-fashioned Fuggles and
Goldings, others say it's simply the
brewer or perhaps they said the brewer
was simple' – and they will arrange
barbecues and such rustic sports as
Milking-the-Goat and Buffy's Leap.
BEERS: Buffy's Bitter, Buffy's Mild,
Polly's Folly, Polly's Xtra Folly, Buffy's
Ale, Buffy's Strong Ale, Festival 9X,
IPA and Hollybeery at Christmas.

ELGOOD

Keen gardeners as well as beer lovers will enjoy a visit to Elgood's elegant Georgian premises alongside the River Nene, for the spacious gardens to the rear of the brewery have been remodelled in Georgian style. The brewery was converted from a mill and a granary and was bought by the Elgood family in 1877. It is still owned by the same family and the three daughters of the present chairman play leading roles in the company, to such an extent that the company name should arguably be changed to 'Elgood and Daughters'. The large brewhouse has superb traditional mash tuns, coppers and high-sided wooden fermenters. Before fermentation, the 'hopped wort' from the coppers is cooled in a large open, shallow copper vessel called a cool ship, still widely used in Belgium but now thought to be unique to Britain. When I asked the head brewer if he ran the risk of wild yeast infection using the open vessel he said 'Not since we cut down the apple trees outside!' The rich and rounded ales, made from Pipkin malt with Challenger and Fuggles whole flower hops, are delivered to forty-five Fenland pubs and to the free trade. BEERS: Black Dog Mild, Cambridge Bitter, Pageant Ale, Golden Newt, Old Black Shuck and Greyhound Strong Bitter plus seasonal ales.

GREENE KING

Greene King is one of England's major regional brewers; an East Anglian giant with more than 1,000 pubs and growing trade throughout southern England. It is based in historic Bury St Edmunds which has many graceful Georgian buildings. Benjamin Greene started to brew in Bury in 1799 and merged with Frederick King's St Edmunds Brewery in 1887. The present brewery was substantially rebuilt in 1939. The brewhouse is superb, based on copper mash tuns and boiling kettles. Hidden away in one part of the brewhouse are two giant wooden vats that store a type of beer which recalls the hey-day of eighteenth-century porter brewing. The vats contain a strong ale of 12 per cent called Old 5X, which is stored for between two and five years, the lids held down by a layer of local soil known as marl. Old 5X is not sold commercially but is used for blending to make Strong Suffolk Ale. The vatted beer is blended with a 5 per cent ale called BPA or Best Pale Ale. The resulting beer is 6 per cent alcohol and has an apple and oak aroma and palate balanced by spicy and peppery hops, with a tart, iodine note in the finish. The beer has been available in bottle for years but in the winter of 1998 it was made available in cask-conditioned form for a limited period. BEERS: XX Dark Mild, IPA, Triumph Bitter and Abbot Ale with a large range of seasonal and occasional beers, including Strong Suffolk Ale.

HIGHWOOD

Tom Wood grew up in a farming community on the edge of the Lincolnshire Wolds where his family grew the finest malting barley. But he had never brewed beer in his life when he got the urge to run his own business, read about the micro-brewing revolution, visited several CAMRA beer festivals, and decided to turn malt into ale. He converted an old granary on the farm where his grandfather and father had stored malting barley, and installed his brewing equipment in 1995. At first he planned to brew and deliver beer on his own but the success of his ales forced him to use the services of his two brothers and finally to employ a professional brewer. The farm supplies him with winter-sown Halcyon barley. Tom brews around forty barrels a week for sixty regular outlets and has bought two local pubs, the Butchers Arms and the Turners Arms.

BEERS: Tom Wood Best Bitter, Shepherd's Delight, Lincolnshire Legend, Harvest Bitter, Bomber County, Jolly Ploughman, Lincolnshire Longwool.

McMULLEN

Peter McMullen, a English country gentleman with some Irish ancestry, founded his brewery in 1827 in the comfortable old county town of Hertford. The red-brick Victorian tower brewery was built on the site of three wells that supply a constant source of fine water for beer-making. The imposing brewhouse is built around traditional circular mash tuns, copper kettles, and oak and copper-lined fermenters. The most interesting of McMullen's malty, fruity ales is called AK, a now rare example of a pale mild. The brewery records do not indicate the origins of the name and a variety of theories have been put forward. The most plausible theory is that the letters were branded on casks in the nineteenth century when breweries made several versions of mild and bitter: A indicates that the beer is the first of McMullen's mild ales, while K, an X cut vertically, singles out milds from stronger bitters, marked with a full X. The company, still controlled by descendants of Peter McMullen, owns 145 pubs in Hertfordshire and surrounding counties and also has a vigorous free trade. As well as AK, its strong winter beer, Stronghart, described as 'liquid Christmas pudding', has won the barley wine class in CAMRA's Champion Winter Beer of Britain competition.

BEERS: Original AK, Country Bitter, Gladstone and Stronghart with several seasonal beers sold under the name of McMullen Special Reserve.

RIDLEY

Thomas Dixon Ridley built his brewery in 1842 in an eighteenth-century mill on the banks of the River Chelmer, a charming rural area of Essex. Ridley was a miller by trade and was encouraged to turn his hand to brewing by his wife, who came from a brewing family in the county town of Chelmsford. Ridley's great-great-grandson, Nicholas, runs the company today and claims an ancestral link with Bishop Nicholas Ridley who was burnt at the stake by Mary I when he refused to renounce his Protestant beliefs. The splendid traditional brewhouse and fermentation room produces cask-conditioned ales of exceptional quality, brewed by a female head brewer, Janina Jones, using Pipkin malts and Fuggles and Goldings whole flower hops. A recent addition to the range, ESX Best, indicates both county pride and the company's support for Essex County Cricket Club.

BEERS: Mild, IPA, ESX Best, Spectacular, Witchfinder Porter, Rumpus and Winter Winner.

St Peter's

St Peter's has one of the finest settings of any small craft brewery, behind an imposing thirteenth-century hall in a remote part of Suffolk. The hall has vaulted ceilings, great inglenook fireplaces, stained-glass mullioned windows, a plethora of beams and memorabilia and artefacts dedicated to St Peter. It is owned by businessman John Murphy who decided to build a brewery in 1996 in order to make beers that would become major international brands. Unlike many micro-breweries that use secondhand vessels, no expense has been spared in installing the finest brewing equipment in converted barns. Pure brewing water is pumped from a well 300 feet beneath the surface and raw materials include Halcyon barley malt, and Challenger and Goldings whole hops. The ever-growing range of beers, draught and packaged, include a raspberry fruit beer and a porter made with the addition of honey. St Peter's owns five pubs in the Waveney Valley area of Suffolk as well as the Jerusalem Tavern in London. The packaged beers come in an eighteenth-century, flagon-shaped bottle, the prototype of which John Murphy found in a shop near Philadelphia in the U.S.A.

BEERS: Fruit Beer, Mild, Wheat Beer, Extra, Golden Ale, Honey Porter and Strong.

TOLLY COBBOLD

Tolly Cobbold is one of the oldest brewing companies in Britain. Its origins lie in a brewery founded in Harwich in 1723 by Thomas Cobbold who moved to Ipswich in 1746 and merged with the local Tollemache Brewery. The fame of the brewery became so great that Ipswich was once known as the town that was 'Cobbold all over'. The present brewery, in a commanding position alongside the River Orwell, was designed by William Bradford using his familiar Victorian tower principle and the great brewing rooms contain some old and beautifully burnished copper vessels. The company was rescued by a management buy-out in 1990 when the property and leisure group Brent Walker planned to close it and turn the brewery into a leisure facility for a yachting marina. The new company owns only one pub, the Brewery Tap in the old head brewer's house in the grounds, but supplies around 400 pubs in the region. The brewery is a major tourist attraction and its Bottlers Room has a collection of 1,800 commemorative bottled beers. When Tolly Cobbold featured in the John Harvey-Jones television series *Troubleshooter*, a special beer called Tollyshooter was brewed to mark the occasion and it has now become a regular member of the portfolio.

BEERS: Mild, Bitter, Original Best Bitter, IPA, Old Strong, Tollyshooter and Conquest plus several seasonal ales.

WOODFORDE'S

Ray Ashworth used to work in a bank and brewed beer at home in his spare time but when he visited a CAMRA beer festival in Norwich in the early 1980s he was convinced that he could brew better beers and was encouraged by his friends to turn his hobby into a commercial venture. He was dogged by misfortune as both of his first two sites were destroyed by fire. But he has thrived since, moving his brewery into converted farm buildings in the picturesque Broadland village of Woodbastwick in 1989. The quality of the ales, brewed with the finest Maris Otter malts and Fuggles and Goldings hops, can be measured by the fact that two of them, Wherry Best Bitter and Headcracker, have both won the Champion Beer of Britain competition. The Fur and Feather pub next to the brewery offers a selection of Woodforde's ales and you can try your hand at brewing them from beer kits available in the brewery shop. The brewery is named after the celebrated Norfolk rector and toper, Parson Woodforde of Reepham.

BEERS: Broadsman Bitter, Wherry Best Bitter, Great Eastern Ale, Nelson's Revenge, Norfolk Nog, Baldric and Norkie plus a wide range of occasional and seasonal ales.

HEART OF ENGLAND

THE CENTRAL BELT of England has had a vital role to play in the development of English beer-making. The small country town of Burton-on-Trent is internationally famous for pale ales that transformed beer long before the arrival of the first golden lagers from Central Europe. The Trent Valley is dotted with springs that provide 'brewing liquor' (water) for the breweries of Burton and neighbouring towns. The water bubbles to the surface through soil rich in such salts as gypsum and magnesium that give a natural sparkle to beer and bring out the best flavours from malt and hops. It was the pale ales of Burton that fashioned a massive export trade in the nineteenth and early twentieth centuries and which, at home, started to challenge the power of the London brewers and their dark porters and stouts. Marston's splendid brewery and its three large rooms packed with wooden 'union set' fermenters recall the pride and pomp of brewing in imperial England. In the nearby Black Country, a curious nineteenth-century blend of belching chimneys and small towns, mild ale brewed in tiny breweries or taverns refreshed legions of thirsty, grimy workers. That tradition survives in the Vine pub and its attached brewery, and at the Beacon Hotel where a powerful dark mild, based on an old recipe, stands as a fascinating reminder of what beer was like earlier in the century. Away from the old industrial areas, Donnington in the Cotswolds enjoys a breathtaking setting while, close to the Welsh border, the Three Tuns brewpub in Bishop's Castle is yet another potent link with brewing's past.

Away from the towns, attempting to cope with a fading industrial base, the vast central area of England has some beautiful countryside. It is fitting that the Vine pub in Brierley Hill welcomes visitors with a quotation from *The Two Gentlemen of Verona*, for the Heart of England is Shakespeare country, much of it dotted with delightful thatched and timber-framed buildings. Derbyshire's Peak District is popular with walkers, climbers and pot-holers. Edale marks the start of the Pennine Way, the spiny backbone of northern England. Nottinghamshire was once a major coal-mining area, immortalised in D. H. Lawrence's novel *Sons and Lovers*; his home in Eastwood is open to the public. Nottingham has its castle and, below, built from the rocks, England's oldest pub, the Trip to Jerusalem, which dates from the time of the Crusades.

ALL NATIONS

The All Nations is an ancient pub that has brewed its own beer for around 200 years and has been run by the Lewis family since 1934. It's known locally as 'Mrs Lewis's' after the mother of the present owner, Keith Lewis. The pub is set in that curious part of Shropshire that is a blend of delightful countryside and the remains of the industrial revolution. It is just off the Ironbridge to Coalport road, names synonymouus with the growth of heavy industry in the nineteenth century. The pub was built at the turn of that century for workers on the adjoining railway line that took coal from Coalport to nearby depots. There are scores of brewpubs in Britain today but the All Nations is one of the few that date from a time before the rise of commercial breweries, when most innkeepers made their own ales. The pub is a listed building and Keith Lewis makes few concessions to the modern world, although he has agreed to serve lunchtime sandwiches in recent years. The one homely bar has lino on the floor and formica on the tables where locals play darts and cribbage. Behind the pub, amid a huddle of outbuildings and a hencoop, the tiny brewery produces just one beer, All Nations Pale Ale. With a modest strength of just 3 per cent alcohol, it is more a light mild than a bitter, and was fashioned to suit the thirsts of workers who were looking for refreshment to wash away hours of grimy labour. Beer: Pale Ale.

BATHAM

Daniel Batham's Black Country pub and brewery is renowned for its fine ale and for its unspoilt Victorian charm. A quotation from Shakespeare's *Two Gentlemen of Verona* is inscribed above the entrance: 'Blessings of Your Heart, You Brew Good Ale'. Daniel Batham opened his pub and brewery in 1877 when he lost his job as a mineworker. He chose the site of a former slaughterhouse and the pub is known locally as the Bull and Bladder even though its official name is the Vine. The company is still run by members of the Batham family, Tim and Matthew, who are fifth generation and supply beer to nine other pubs. The brewery is small and cramped, with splendid Victorian mash tuns, coppers and open fermenters. For many years, Batham produced only mild ale in the Black Country tradition for an army of thirsty miners and foundry workers. But changing times have seen bitter overtake mild to such an extent that the brewery makes just one 'parti-gyle' beer, with additional brewing liquor added to take the bitter down from 4.3 per cent to 3.5 per cent alcohol. Caramel is then blended in to give the mild its colour. The beers can be enjoyed in the comfort of either the locals' front bar of the pub, a new lounge that was added in 1996 or a large back bar where live jazz concerts are staged at weekends. BEERS: Mild and Bitter plus a Christmas ale.

BELVOIR

A craft brewery set up in 1995 in the lovely Vale of Belvoir in Leicestershire. The owners help unravel the mysteries of English place-name pronounciation by helpfully calling one of their beers Beaver Bitter. The brewhouse is set in a converted cattle shed on a farm and, unlike many craft breweries, has proper equipment as much of it was bought from large regional breweries including Home, Hardys and Hansons, and the closed Victorian brewery of Shipstone's in Nottingham. Brewer Colin Brown worked for Shipstone's and his Star Bitter replicates both the flavour of the old Nottingham ale and the symbol of the brewery. His vessels, including a Shipstone's conditioning tank turned into a copper, are attractively wood-clad. He uses Maris Otter malt and hops from Worcestershire. The brewery has a pub in Nottingham called the Beaver Tap named by Colin Brown who said 'It's the brewery tap, the closest to the brewery even though it's twenty miles away!'
BEERS: Whippling Golden Bitter, Star Bitter, High Flyer and Beaver Bitter with seasonal and occasional ales.

BURTON BRIDGE

The Burton Bridge craft brewery is in the famous brewing town of Burton-on-Trent, the home of English pale ale. The brewery was set up behind the Bridge Inn by Geoff Mumford and Bruce Wilkinson in 1982. An old Victorian building behind the inn was converted to take the brewing equipment. Using the famous hard brewing 'liquor' from the springs of the Trent Valley, where deposits of gypsum and magnesium salts make the water ideal for producing pale ales, Geoff and Bruce fashioned rich and tangy beers with uncompromising malt and hops flavours. Their Burton Bridge Porter is available in bottle-fermented as well as draught form and bottles come with a hand-painted label. Empire Pale Ale, at 7.5 per cent, is also bottle-fermented, and won the *Guardian*/CAMRA award of Champion Bottle-Conditioned Beer in 1997 as well as runner-up in the same competition a year later. The beer recalls the strong India Pale Ales made in Burton in the nineteenth century for the colonial trade. The beers can be enjoyed in the Bridge Inn with its wooden pews and walls decorated with the brewery's many awards. A traditional skittles alley is attached to the pub.
BEERS: Summer Ale, XL Bitter, Bridge Bitter, Burton Bridge Porter, Staffordshire Knot Brown, Top Dog Stout, Festival Ale, Old Expensive and Empire Pale Ale (bottle-fermented) and several seasonal and occasional beers.

THE ECCLESHALL BREWERY

The brewery with its ten-barrel equipment is in outbuildings behind the George Hotel, run by the Slater family. Andrew Slater's parents installed the brewing equipment in 1995 to give an added dimension to the pub's business and then encouraged him to learn the brewing skills on some specialist courses. Andrew brews with Halcyon malts and Challenger and Whitbread Goldings Variety hops. The George is a former coaching inn with heavy beams, an open fire in a large brick inglenook and many old prints decorating the walls. Accommodation is available.
BEERS: Slaters Bitter, Slater Original, Top Totty, Slaters Premium and Organ Grinder.

ENVILLE

Enville has turned the clock back to the days when farmer-brewers used the natural ingredients which were available to them to make ale. In the case of Enville, based in a delightful complex of Victorian farm buildings, honey is added to the beers. Around three tons of honey, produced on the farm, is used every year, which also grows its own Maris Otter barley for malting. Owner Will Cort planned to produce honey commercially, with brewing as a sideline, but the success of his beers reduced the bees to a walk-on part in the enterprise. Enville supplies some eighty outlets with beer hopped with Challenger, Fuggles and East Kent Goldings. Will uses the same water source as a brewery in the same village that closed in 1919 and uses recipes handed down by his great-great-aunt. His Simpkiss Bitter replicates the beer from a renowned Black Country brewery that closed in the 1970s.
BEERS: Bitter, Low Gravity Mild, Simpkiss Bitter, White, Ale and Gothic.

FARMERS ARMS MAYHEM'S BREW HOUSE

This tiny brewery in an attractive thatched barn in the grounds of the Farmers Arms pub was opened in 1992 and was bought by Wadworth of Devizes four years later. As well as two beers available only in the pub, the brewery also makes its own cider. Odda's Light is a golden pale ale with a good balance of malt and hops on the aroma and palate and a bitter finish while Mayhem's Sundowner is a smooth strong bitter with a biscuity malt character and a bitter-sweet finish.
BEERS: Odda's Light and Mayhem's Sundowner.

GRAINSTORE

Grainstore has a superb setting in a restored Victorian railway building alongside Oakham station in England's smallest county of Rutland. The company that owns the brewery goes by the odd name of Davis'es Brewing taking its name from founders Tony Davis and Mike Davies. Tony Davis enjoyed a thirty-year career in brewing, ending with Ruddles, just a couple of miles from Oakham in the village of Langham. When he left Ruddles he planned to run his own craft brewery and tap room and went into business with Mike Davies in 1995. The tap room, or bar, in the brewery building sells the beers along with some sixty other pubs in the area. Cooking, the name of the brewery's 3.6 per cent bitter, comes from the nickname given by brewers to their standard bitters or cooking bitters, an ironic play on the term 'cooking sherry'. Grainstore also brews Tupping Ale for the British Charollais Sheep Society: Tup is a dialect word for a sheep.

BEERS: Cooking, Triple B, Springtime, Gold, Harvest IPA, Ten Fifty and Winter Oats.

HARDYS AND HANSONS

On the outskirts of Nottingham in a dormitory village, the imposing red-brick Victorian brewery dominates the area. The Hardy and Hanson breweries were established respectively in 1832 and 1847 but merged in 1931. The company is still controlled by members of the ruling families and the brewery has classic brewing vessels. Until the decline of the mining industry, Kimberley Ales were supplied mainly to scores of coal miners' pubs and clubs but the brewery has had to refashion its business since the 1980s, adding a bitter and hoppy/fruity Kimberley Classic to its flagship, easy-drinking mild and bitter, along with several seasonal and occasional brews. All the beers have complex hop recipes, using Challenger, Goldings, Northdown, Styrian Goldings and Target varieties. A few yards from the brewery, the ales can be enjoyed in the Nelson and Railway, once two pubs alongside Kimberley railway station that have been knocked into one, with a wood-panelled bar and a beamed lounge. The brewery also owns the Trip to Jerusalem, the oldest inn in England and built into the rock on which Nottingham Castle stands.
BEERS: Kimberley Best Mild, Best Bitter and Classic plus such seasonal ales as Crazy Cow, Crowing Cock, Frolicking Farmer, Peddler's Pride, Guzzling Goose and Rocking Rudolph.

HOBSONS

Hobsons has made a point of locating in fine buildings. It opened in 1993 in a former sawmill and moved to a former farm granary. The brewery produces sixty barrels of beer a week, delivered to around eighty pubs. Maris Otter malt and Challenger, Fuggles, Goldings and Target whole flower hops give rich, full-bodied aromas and flavours to the beer. Best Bitter won a gold award in the 1997 Champion Beer of Britain competition. A quirk in the post system means that while the brewery's address places it in Worcestershire it is geographically in Shropshire.
BEERS: Best Bitter, Town Crier and Old Henry.

SARAH HUGHES

If you want to know what mild ale tasted like in its hey-day then you should visit the Beacon Hotel in Sedgley. The tiny but classic tower brewery attached to the hotel had been idle and derelict for thirty years when the owner, John Hughes, found his grandmother's recipe for mild ale in a cigar box among her effects stored in a bank vault. Most of the old brewing vessels had rotted away and John had to replace them with modern ones from former West Midlands breweries, including Ansells of Birmingham. The mashing begins the brewing process in a small cramped room at the top of the brewhouse which is reached by clambering up narrow stairs. From there the sweet extract flows down one floor to the copper where it is boiled with hops. Finally, the beer is fermented on the ground floor. Sarah Hughes' Dark Ruby Mild is brewed from Maris Otter pale and crystal malts, and Fuggles and Goldings hops. The most amazing thing about this mild beer is its strength – 6 per cent alcohol. Earlier in the century the term mild was not synonymous with weak but merely meant that the style was less heavily hopped than pale ale or bitter. The mild brewed at the Beacon Hotel bursts with amazing flavours of dark malt, tannins and bitter fruit, underpinned by a spicy and resiny hoppiness.

BEERS: Pale Amber, Sedgley Surprise and Dark Ruby Mild. Dark Ruby Mild is also available bottle-fermented.

MANSFIELD

Mansfield is a large commercial brewery in an industrial town but is included in this book as a result of its adherence to a fermenting system known as the Yorkshire square method. A Yorkshire square is a two-storey vessel with a porthole in the centre. Fermentation begins in the lower storey and yeast and carbon dioxide carry the liquid through the porthole to the top storey. A raised rim around the hole captures the yeast while the liquid runs back into the lower storey. Like the Burton union method (see Marston's) the system was devised to cleanse pale ale of yeast. Mansfield was founded in 1855 and for most of its life supplied miners' pubs and clubs around the Nottinghamshire pits. It has had to refashion its business and now owns close to 500 pubs. A new brewhouse, using modern, stainless steel mash tuns, coppers and fermenters was built to cope with demand. The beers are brewed from Halcyon malts and hopped with Fuggles and Styrian Goldings. The strong Old Baily is named after a former brewery executive and has no connection with London's famous court house of the same, differently spelt, name.

BEERS: Riding Mild, Riding Bitter, Mansfield Bitter and Old Baily plus seasonal ales.

MARSTON'S

Marston, Thompson and Evershed's brewery is a treasure house of splendid Victorian brewing vessels. The centrepiece is the Burton union system of fermentation, once widespread in Burton but now unique to Marston's. Three vast rooms are packed with large wooden casks linked together ('held in union') by pipes and troughs. Brewing starts in a conventional way, with a mash being made and the sweet wort boiled with hops in coppers. Fermentation gets under way in shallow open vessels but after a day or two the liquid is pumped to the union casks. Here the liquid is driven out of the casks and up swan-necked pipes by yeast and carbon dioxide. It drips into barm troughs above the casks (barm is a dialect word for yeast) where the yeast is trapped while the liquid runs back into the casks. The system was developed in the nineteenth century when pale ale became fashionable in Burton. The rise of pale ale coincided with commercial glass making: consumers could see the beer in their glasses and demanded a clear drink free from dregs. The union system was devised to cleanse fermenting beer of yeast but in so doing created a beer that was remarkably

delicate and subtle in flavour yet with good malt and hop character. Marston's moved to its present site when the London brewer Mann Crossman and Paulin left Burton to return to the capital. From the malt store at the top of the brewery there are fine views over the Trent Valley which is dotted with springs that provide the sparkling hard waters needed by brewers to produce pale ale. Marston's major brand is called Pedigree Bitter but it is a true example of a Burton pale ale that revolutionized brewing on a world scale. The company is so committed to the union system that the third room of oak casks (made from German wood and built in Scotland) was installed in 1992 at a cost of more than £1 million. The yeast from the union sets is used to ferment all Marston's beers: the characteristic sulphury aroma of the beers comes from the yeast and the gypsum salts in the brewing water. The aroma is known locally as 'The Burton snatch'. The beers are brewed from pale malt, glucose sugar and Fuggles, Goldings and Whitbread Goldings Variety.
BEERS: Bitter, Pedigree Bitter and Owd Rodger plus a vast range of seasonal ales. Oyster Stout is available in bottle-fermented form.

SHUGBOROUGH

Shugborough, with Traquair House in Scotland, is a now rare example of a manor house brewery, recalling the time when most stately homes had small breweries to supply the family and servants with ale: in many cases the head butler acted as the brewer. Shugborough's brewery is at Shugborough Hall, seat of the earls of Lichfield, and is set in part of the buildings that also house the Staffordshire County Museum. The tiny brewery had not been used for decades when Keith Bott, owner of the Titanic Brewery in Stoke-on-Trent, was given permission to brew there for demonstration purposes. It is run by log fires that heat the minuscule mash tun and copper. The beers, available on draught and in bottle-fermented form, became so popular that they are now on sale commercially. They are brewed from Maris Otter pale malt with amber, crystal and wheat malts. English Fuggles and Goldings are the main hop varieties but American Galena and Willamette are used in Longhorn.
BEERS: Longhorn, Horsepower, Redcap and Saddleball.

TEME VALLEY

Teme Valley is all about hops and the Clift family have grown hops in the Malvern Hills for 150 years. In 1997 they decided to add a small micro-brewery to the rear of their delightful Talbot inn. From the small brewery in converted outbuildings, it is just a few yards to the bars of the Talbot, where the beams and ceilings are decorated with fresh hops from the surrounding fields. The beers, not surprisingly, burst with fresh and tangy hop flavours and are available in three other local pubs. The Talbot is famous for the quality of its food, using organic ingredients grown on its farm and gardens. The beamed inn, with ancient settles, offers accommodation. The pub and brewery are close to Edward Elgar's home, which is open to the public.
BEERS: The Other T'Other, This, That and Wot.

JOHN THOMPSON

The John Thompson is a fine inn with a brewery attached: the beers are brewed under the name of Lloyds Country Beers for both the inn and around 150 other pubs in the area. The beers are made from Maris Otter pale malt, with some chocolate malt in the stronger brews. The main hop variety is Challenger, with Target and American Willamette. The beers are notably fruity and bitter with a touch of sulphur on the aroma: fresh supplies of yeast are brought regularly from Burton-on-Trent for fermentation. The beers can be enjoyed in the inn with its ceiling joists, beams and old oak settles: it has a superb setting, with gardens overlooking the sweep of the River Trent.
Beers: Derby Bitter or JTS XXX, IPA (Ingleby Pale Ale), Scratching Dog, Vixen Velvet and VIP (Very Important Pint).

THREE TUNS

This is a Victorian tower brewery on a lilliputian scale at the back of the Three Tuns pub in the attractive border town of Bishop's Castle. The four-storey building has malt store and liquor tanks at the top, with mash tun, copper and fermenters ranged on the floors below. The brewery retains many of its Victorian vessels. From the malt store you can step on the floor of the hoist and marvel at the superb sweep of the surrounding countryside and low, misty hills, where England becomes Wales. It was run for many years by a legendary brewer-cum-innkeeper called John Roberts. The brewery and pub closed in the mid-1990s and was rescued by a group of local people determined to maintain the traditions of good ale and fine food at the Three Tuns. The unspoilt pub has several small rooms with wooden floors, settles and open fires.
Beers: Sexton, XXX Bitter, Offa's Ale and Roberts' Winter Special plus two bottle-fermented ales Cleric's Cure and Old Scrooge.

The Three Tuns

A licence to brew and sell beer was probably first granted here in 1642. The present Tower Brewery was built in the 1880's by John Roberts. The famous XXX bitter is still brewed to the original recipe and still sold at the adjoining Three Tuns Inn.

March 27th 1899

My Dear Roberts

I hope you will not forget to send some beer tomorrow (Tuesday) as I have not had a glass since I last saw you. Please send it good, as I shall have the Bishop and some of the Clergy here on Tuesday week and you know there are no people in the world better judges of drink than they are. I want them to be able to exclaim as with one voice, after they have tasted your beer, "Roberts, deserves well of his Country as he is the only man who has discovered a CURE for agricultural depression".

Yours truly

(Revd.)

THREE TUNS BREWERY
FINE OLD ALES BREWED THE TRADITIONAL WAY
Cleric's Cure
Bitter Beer
XXX
BOTTLE CONDITIONED
BISHOP'S CASTLE

500ml ℮
5% ABV
The Three Tuns Brewing Co. Ltd.
Salop St., Bishop's Castle
Shropshire
SY9 5BW

BEST BEFORE:

5 034240 000136

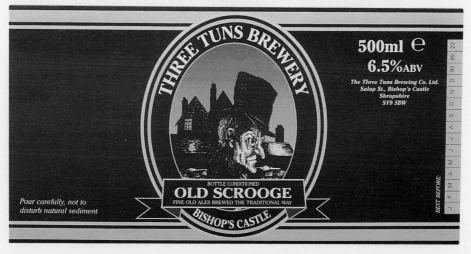

THREE TUNS BREWERY
BOTTLE CONDITIONED
OLD SCROOGE
FINE OLD ALES BREWED THE TRADITIONAL WAY
BISHOP'S CASTLE

Pour carefully, not to disturb natural sediment

500ml ℮
6.5% ABV
The Three Tuns Brewing Co. Ltd.
Salop St., Bishop's Castle
Shropshire
SY9 5BW

BEST BEFORE:

WHEATSHEAF INN AND FROMES HILL BREWERY

The Wheatsheaf is home to the Fromes Hill Brewery where Peter Mirfin brews by the side of the pub in a small plant established in 1993. The previous owner of the pub installed the brewery but lost interest in making beer. He took Peter on to brew and he ended buying the pub as well. He produces two beers using Maris Otter pale malt and small amounts of crystal malt. Challenger, Fuggles and Goldings hops are grown locally. The beers can be enjoyed in the single-bar, open-plan pub which has some exposed stonework. BEERS: Buckswood Dingle and Overture.

WHIM

Whim is a farm brewery, recalling the times when many farmers made beer to refresh families and labourers, especially at harvest time, using barley and other cereals from the surrounding fields. Whim was opened in 1993 in redundant farm buildings by Giles Litchfield who now also owns the Broughton brewery in Scotland. Using Maris Otter malt and Goldings hops, the beers are available in some sixty pubs and the brewery has its own outlet, the Wilkes Head in Leek.

BEERS: Arbor Light, Magic Mushroom Mild, Hartington Bitter, Hartington IPA and Special Ale, plus seasonal and occasional ales. Black Bear Extra Stout is sold in bottle-fermented form.

WICKWAR

Wickwar has a glorious location in the old coopers' shop at the former Arnold, Perret & Co. brewery, which also housed a cider mill, demonstrating the importance of the juice of the barley and the apple in this part of the country. The brewery opened on what the owners call 'The glorious first of May 1990' when the government introduced 'the Guest Beer Order' that enabled the tenants of pubs owned by national brewers to buy a cask-conditioned ale free of the tie. The brewers were also tenants of three Courage pubs and they brewed with a view to just supplying their pubs. But their beers became so popular that they left the pub trade to concentrate solely on brewing and they now supply some 150 pubs. The beers are made with Halcyon pale, crystal and chocolate malts and are hopped with Challenger and Fuggles varieties. The recipe for Station Porter is a secret and the brewers are rightly proud of this remarkable ale with its rich coffee and roasted malt flavours. The beer, bottle-fermented as well as on draught, won a silver award in 1997 and 1998 in the Champion Beer of Britain competition. BEERS: Coopers' WPA (Wickwar Pale Ale), Brands Oak Bitter (BOB), Old Merryford Ale and Station Porter.

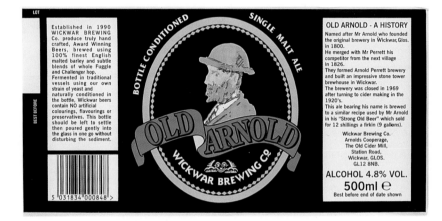

Established in 1990 WICKWAR BREWING Co. produce truly hand crafted, Award Winning Beers, brewed using 100% finest English malted barley and subtle blends of whole Fuggle and Challenger hop. Fermented in traditional vessels using our own strain of yeast and naturally conditioned in the bottle, Wickwar beers contain NO artificial colourings, flavourings or preservatives. This bottle should be left to settle then poured gently into the glass in one go without disturbing the sediment.

BOTTLE CONDITIONED
SINGLE MALT ALE

OLD ARNOLD
WICKWAR BREWING Cº

OLD ARNOLD - A HISTORY
Named after Mr Arnold who founded the original brewery in Wickwar, Glos. in 1800.
He merged with Mr Perrett his competitor from the next village in 1826.
They formed Arnold Perrett brewery and built an impressive stone tower brewhouse in Wickwar.
The brewery was closed in 1969 after turning to cider making in the 1920's.
This ale bearing his name is brewed to a similar recipe used by Mr Arnold in his "Strong Old Beer" which sold for 12 shillings a firkin (9 gallons).

Wickwar Brewing Co.
Arnolds Cooperage,
The Old Cider Mill,
Station Road,
Wickwar, GLOS.
GL12 8NB.

ALCOHOL 4.8% VOL.
500ml ℮
Best before end of date shown

WOOD

The brothers Anthony and Edward Wood and their father Basil launched their brewery in 1980 in fine old brick-built stables next to their Plough Inn in a village in the gently rolling Shropshire hills. The success of the beers, which are supplied to around 200 pubs, has meant that the brewery has more than doubled in size. In 1991 the Woods added the Sam Powell range of Welsh beers to their portfolio when that brewery ceased trading. The beer range is now vast and includes many seasonal ales, made from pale, crystal and chocolate malts and hopped with traditional Fuggles and Goldings varieties. The countryside around Wistanstow was made famous by A.E. Housman in his many poems, notably *A Shropshire Lad* and the brewery launched an ale of that name as a seasonal brew but it is now made all year round.
BEERS: Wallop, Sam Powell Best Bitter, Sam Powell Original Bitter, Summer That!, Parish Bitter, Special Bitter, Shropshire Lad, Sam Powell Old Sam and Wonderful plus seasonal beers for each month of the year. Shropshire Lad is available in bottle-fermented form.

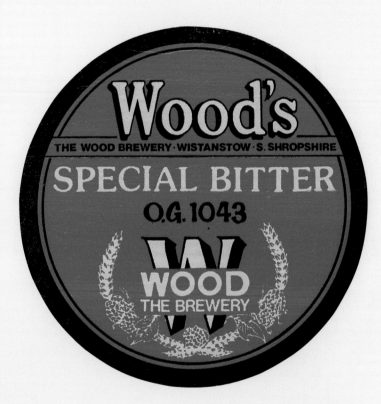

Yorkshire and North-east England

Black Sheep,
Yorkshire

Yorkshire, with a proud and insular population that looks down on southern beers, has its own idiosyncratic approach to brewing. Yorkshire beer, famously, comes with a thick head of foam. The foam today can be created by all manner of devices in brewery and pub cellar, including the use of nitrogen gas or by aerating the beer as it is poured by forcing it through a tight 'sparkler' attached to the pump. Historically, though, the high level of natural carbon dioxide in beer was the result of fermenting it in stone or slate fermenters known as 'Yorkshire squares' with a yeast strain that worked slowly and had to be regularly stirred into action by pumping oxygen into it. Modern squares, made from stainless steel, can be seen in such vast beer factories as Tetley's in Leeds, but the original stone type still operate in the Black Sheep Brewery in the Dales and at Samuel Smith's fiercely traditionalist brewery in Tadcaster, where coopers fashion wooden casks and local deliveries are made by horse-drawn drays. Further north, there is a a tribal loyalty to beers known as 'Scotch', so named for the very good reason that they were first brewed in Scotland and 'exported' over the border into Northumberland and Durham. The Castle Eden Brewery in County Durham, ear-marked for closure by Whitbread, and then saved by a local management rescue at the time of writing, was famous for its Scotch Bitter under its original name of Nimmos, and it is hoped that, free and independent once again, it will resurrect the name and the style.

Tadcaster, known as 'the Burton of the North', is a small town with a big brewing tradition. As well as the two Smith breweries, there is also an outpost of the Bass empire, though its processed 'keg' beers are not worthy of mention. Yorkshire offers magnificent countryside, including the Moors and the Dales, while its many old monasteries and abbeys recall the time when monks were at the centre of brewing. Rievaulx means 'rye valley' and is the grandest of the Cistercian abbeys in the region. The monks chose the site for both its solitude and the quality of the local water for brewing. Yorkshire has a spectacular coastline, including Robin Hood's Bay and Whitby with its Dracula connections. Further north, both countryside and coastline become ever more wild and rugged; Northumberland has some fine castles, notably the beautifully maintained Bamburgh Castle.

BLACK SHEEP

The Black Sheep Brewery is one of the most remarkable success stories in brewing in recent years. Paul Theakston worked for several years for the family-owned brewery of that name in the Yorkshire Dales market town of Masham (pronounced 'Massum'). When the company was bought by brewing giant Scottish and Newcastle, Paul decided to leave. But beer was in his blood and in 1992 he opened his own brewery in the former Wellgarth maltings in Masham. The area is famous for its black-faced sheep and when Paul was trying to think of a name for his brewery his wife, Sue, remarked 'You'll be the black sheep of the family when you go into competition with Theakstons.' The name immediately caught on and seven years later Paul Theakston is brewing a thousand barrels of beer a week, supplied to some 400 hundred pubs in the region. The brewery is in mellow stone buildings and the equipment is highly traditional, with mash tuns, coppers and Yorkshire square fermenters made of slate. The ales are notably fruity and hoppy, brewed with Maris Otter malts and Challenger, Fuggles, Goldings and Progress whole flower hops. The name of the strong bitter, Riggwelter, comes from a Dales dialect word meaning a sheep that has fallen on its back.
BEERS: Black Sheep Best Bitter, Special Bitter and Riggwelter.

BORDER

Border Brewery occupies the kiln room of the former, long-closed brewery of the same name that dated from 1894, was bought by Vaux of Sunderland in 1934 and closed three years later. The premises were bought in 1980 by Alan and Carol Crawford for use as a joinery but they decided to open a small brewery in 1992. In 1994 they leased the brewery to Andrew Burrows and Leslie Orde. The brick-built kiln was part of the old brewery's maltings: when the barley had germinated, with starches beginning the change into malt sugar, it was loaded into the kiln and heated over wood fires. The present small plant uses Maris Otter malts and Challenger, Fuggles, Goldings and Styrian Goldings hops for beers bursting with biscuity malt and spicy, resiny hop character. The brewery owns one pub and supplies 150 further outlets. It produces ten to twelve barrels of draught beer a week and 500 bottles.
BEERS: Farne Island Pale Ale, Flotsam Bitter, Old Kiln Ale, Noggins Nog, Jetsam Bitter and SOB.

CASTLE EDEN

Although it is in the heart of the old Durham coal field and pit villages, Castle Eden has an almost sylvan air. Its whitewashed buildings look like a stable block from the outside and it stands opposite a pleasant green. The brewery, which takes its name from the surrounding village, has its roots in an inn called the Castle that brewed ale at the junction of the Durham, Newcastle and Sunderland roads in the eighteenth century. In 1826 John Nimmo arrived in Castle Eden from Newcastle, bought the inn and developed it into a brewery. The Nimmos became famous for their mild, porter and pale ale but their flagship beer was a Scotch, a north-east speciality brewed with roasted barley. The Nimmo reign lasted until 1963 when the company was bought by the giant national brewing group Whitbread, which announced in 1998 that it planned to close the site. Brewery manager Jim Kerr found new business partners and raised the funds to buy the brewery from Whitbread in the autumn of 1998. The brewhouse is superb, with wood-jacketed mash tuns, copper kettles and open square fermenters. There are many Nimmo artefacts on the site, including the family crest etched into the doors of the entrance. Beer: Castle Eden Ale Nimmos XXXX.

CROPTON

Cropton began life in 1984 as a tiny brewery in the cellar of the New Inn. It was designed to supply just the inn with ale but demand led first to an expansion in the cellar and then into a purpose-built new brewery behind the pub. The ales are all additive-free and come in bottle-fermented as well as cask-conditioned form, made from pale and coloured malts and Challenger and Goldings whole hops, with the exception of Uncle Sam's, which uses American Cascade hops that impart a stunning citrus fruit character to the beer. Scoresby Stout, which uses roasted barley, is one of the finest of the revivalist stouts. The beers are available in some fifty local pubs and can be enjoyed next to the brewery in the New Inn with its church panels, a plethora of brass and open fires. Accommodation is available and the bottled versions of the beers can be bought in six-packs.
BEERS: King Billy, Two Pints, Scoresby Stout, Uncle Sam's, Backwoods Bitter and Monkmans Slaughter.

DALESIDE

A small brewery with a big reputation, Daleside started life as the Big End Brewery in the mid-1980s but moved to new premises and changed its name at the same time in 1992. It now sells beer to some 200 pubs in Yorkshire, Northumbria and as far south as London and Kent. The beers are uncompromisingly malty, roasty and bitter. Morocco Ale is a recreation of a beer once brewed at Levens Hall in Lancashire 300 years ago and matured for long periods. The ale is spiced, and has a massive aroma and flavour of root ginger balanced by dark, fruity malt and tangy hops. Both Morocco Ale and the malty-roasty Monkey Wrench have won top prizes in the Champion Beer of Britain competition. The beers are brewed with pale and crystal malts and are hopped with Challenger and Goldings varieties.

BEERS: Nightjar, Country Stile, Old Lubrication, Green Grass Old Rogue Ale, Crack Shot, Monkey Wrench and Morocco Ale.

HAMBLETON

Nick Stafford started to brew in 1991 in a Victorian barn on the banks of the River Swale. The success of his beers forced a move to new premises at the other end of the hamlet in 1996 and production quickly reached fifty barrels a week. The company was boosted in 1997 when it won the first-ever Champion Winter Beer of Britain competition, staged by CAMRA, with Nightmare Porter, fashioned from Halcyon pale malt, chocolate malt and roast barley with Northdown whole flower hops. A bottling line was installed in 1997. Nick Stafford is a leading member of the Society of Independent Brewers: he is the current treasurer and takes an active part in the society's campaign with the government for lower rates of excise duty for small breweries.

BEERS: Bitter, Goldfield, Stallion, Stud and Nightmare Porter.

HIGH FORCE

This is England's highest brewery, standing more than 1,000 feet above sea level. The brewery, started by Graeme and Caroline Baxter, takes its name from both the hotel it serves and the magnificent waterfalls that are a major tourist attraction in a lovely area of pine woods and high moors. The hotel offers accommodation and doubles as a mountain rescue centre. At the end of 1998 the Baxters sold the hotel and brewery and bought Yates Brewery in Cumbria (see page 133).
BEERS: Low Force, Teesdale Bitter, Forest XB and Cauldron Snout. Cauldron Snout is also available in bottle-fermented form.

JOHN SMITH

Tadcaster is a small country town near York unusual for the fact that it has two breweries named Smith.

John Smith's Brewery is the last word in high-tech brewing. At the turn of the twentieth century, a row in the Smith family led to John Smith walking up the hill and building a rival brewery. Unlike the rather squat, original brewery building that had been extended over the years, John Smith's plant was a fine example of late Victorian architecture, resplendent with vast brewing rooms, great arched windows and a commanding chimney. But eventually, John Smith's became part of the national Courage brewing group which in turn was merged with Scottish and Newcastle to become Scottish Courage. The brewery has lost its original vessels and the entire brewing process now takes place in stainless steel equipment and with fermentation in conical vessels rather than Yorkshire squares. Standing almost side by side, the two breweries offer fascinating examples of the old and the new in British brewing.
BEERS: John Smith's Bitter and Magnet.

SAMUEL SMITH

The Samuel Smith site is the oldest brewery in Yorkshire, built in 1758. It relishes its antiquity, serving its cask ale from wooden casks, employing coopers to mend the casks, and making local deliveries by horse-drawn drays. The centrepiece of the brewery is its Yorkshire square fermenters made of slate. The slate keeps the beer cool during fermentation while the two-storeyed vessels enable yeast to be removed from the liquid and help develop a high level of natural carbonation that gives the finished beer the thick collar of foam demanded by Northern drinkers. The beers are made from pale and coloured malts with Fuggles and Goldings hops. Samuel Smith has phased out the use of brewing sugars and claims that its lager meets the strict demands of the German Reinheitsgebot – the Pure Beer Law.

BEERS: Old Brewery Bitter plus some magnificent bottled beers including Taddy Porter and Imperial Stout.

TIMOTHY TAYLOR

Timothy Taylor was a maltster who decided, logically, to use his malt and make beer. He began brewing in Keighley (pronounced 'Keethley') in 1858 and moved to the Knowle Spring site in 1863. The mellow brick buildings are supplied by Pennine brewing water from the spring which is so pure that Tim Taylor's grandson, John Taylor (now Lord Ingrow) takes home supplies of the water to mix with his whisky. The remarkable aromas and flavours of the beers, produced in splendidly traditional vessels, are the result of an unusual blend of ingredients. The brewery uses Scottish Golden Promise malt. While some darker crystal malt is used in the Best Bitter, both Golden Best and Landlord are made entirely from pale Golden Promise malt with no brewing sugars or other grains added. Whole flower hops are Fuggles and Goldings with Styrian Goldings from Slovenia used for aroma. After the copper boil, Landlord is allowed to circulate over a deep bed of Styrian Goldings to enrich the aroma and flavour. Landlord, which has three times been named Champion Beer of Britain by CAMRA, is an astonishingly complex ale with a fragrant citrus fruit character.

BEERS: Golden Best, Dark Mild, Porter, Best Bitter, Landlord and Ram Tam.

THEAKSTON

Theakston is a name redolent with brewing history but the brewery has led a chequered existence in recent years since it was taken over by the giant Scottish Courage group. The brewery was founded in the Black Bull pub in 1827 and moved to its present site, complete with its own maltings, in Masham in 1875. In the 1920s it merged with another Masham brewer called Lightfoot. Brewing takes place in splendid old vessels, including a cast-iron mash tun with an oak jacket, an open cool ship pan for cooling the wort, and rooms packed with high-sided wooden fermenters. Tours of the brewery include a small museum dedicated to brewing life, the centre of which is a coopers' shop where wooden casks are still fashioned by skilled craftsmen – obscuring the fact that most of Theakston's ales are now made in a large beer factory on Tyneside. The brewery's most famous beer, Old Peculier, is a fine example of a rich, full-bodied old ale. The curious name and spelling derive from Norman times when Masham was a centre of the wool trade and was allowed a degree of independence from the bishops of York. The town was permitted to control its own Church court, which was known as a 'peculier', outside the jurisdiction of bishops.

BEERS: Mild Ale, Black Bull Bitter, Best Bitter, XB and Old Peculier plus several seasonal ales.

North-west England and the Lakes

WITH THE EXCEPTION of Lees brewery, which is on the outer fringe of the city, Manchester does not figure in a book about country breweries. But it exerts a powerful influence on the north-west, not least because it remains a great brewing centre, with four large commercial breweries and a fifth in neighbouring Stockport. The style is a complex one, with tangy, creamy malt vying for attention with an uncompromising hop bitterness. It is a style that owes a great deal to the history of the region where refreshment and nourishment were demanded by drinkers after long stints in mines and mills. Liverpool, of course, has made its own influence felt. The presence of a large Irish population meant that Irish stout was sent from Dublin to Liverpool and Merseyside brewers responded with their own dark beers, including dark milds rich in roasted malt and tangy hop flavours. It is a heritage that explains the survival of mild in the north-west when it has disappeared from most other parts of the country. The breweries represented here include Burtonwood, which has had to rebuild its business following the collapse of the local mining industry, Coniston in a beautiful setting in the heart of the Lakes, and Jennings which stands proud beneath the protecting bulk of Cockermouth Castle.

The region is most famous for the tranquil beauty of the Lake District. Compressed and squeezed by geological eruptions at the dawn of history, the district is tiny yet appears large as a result of the height of the mountains and the awesome depths of the lakes. It has inspired writers and poets, ranging from Wordsworth to the children's authors Beatrix Potter and Arthur Ransome: Wordsworth's homes at Grasmere and Rydal Mount are open to the public, as is Beatrix Potter's house at Hill Top Farm, Near Sawrey. Ransome, sensibly, lived and worked for a time in a cottage near a pub, the Masons Arms at Cartmel Fell. There are ferries and cruisers on Windermere and Coniston Water while the 'Laal Ratty' Ravenglass to Eskdale steam railway runs through seven miles of enchanted countryside in the Esk Valley.

BURTONWOOD

Burtonwood Brewery was founded in 1867 by James Forshaw and is still controlled by the Dutton-Forshaw family. Although it is now a suburb of Warrington, Burtonwood was a small village that was once the heart of the local mining industry. The brewery's trade for decades was in mineworkers' clubs and pubs. When that market disappeared, £6 million was pumped into rebuilding and refashioning the company's image and beer style. A new brewhouse was installed in the 1990s and is a good example of modern brewing design, with large stainless steel mash tuns, coppers and closed fermenters in a big, airy environment. The beers have a rich, creamy malt character balanced by complex hop bitterness from Challenger, Fuggles, Goldings and Progress varieties. Burtonwood owns close to 500 pubs and in 1998 went into partnership with the Thomas Hardy Brewery in Dorchester to pool brewing resources and seek contracts from pub groups for 'house beers'.
BEERS: Mild, Bitter, James Forshaw's Bitter, Top Hat and Buccaneer.

CONISTON

Ian Bradley set up his ten-barrel brewery in 1995 behind his father's pub, the Black Bull. It is an idyllic setting, at the foot of Coniston Old Man mountain and a short walk from Coniston Water where Donald Campbell met his death in 1967 attempting to break the world water-speed record in his boat, *Bluebird*. The Black Bull was Campbell's base for his ill-fated expedition and, not surprisingly, the brewery's main beer is called Bluebird. Rather more surprisingly, Bluebird Bitter won the top prize in the 1998 Champion Beer of Britain competition, plunging the small, remote brewery into national prominence. Brewed from Maris Otter pale and crystal malts, with a generous dose of Challenger hops, and pure mountain water, the beer has a luscious malt and tangy, fruity hop character. Opium is a reference to certain substances enjoyed by the notorious Lakeland set of artists and writers. To meet demand, a bottled version of Bluebird was brewed for Coniston in 1998 by Brakspear of Henley-on-Thames.

BEERS: Bluebird Bitter, Opium, Old Man Ale and Blacksmith's Ale.

DENT

The village of Dent is in disputed territory: it is officially in Cumbria but stands in what are called locally the 'Yorkshire' Dales. The small brewery was set up in 1990 in a barn behind the Sun Inn to supply the Sun and two other pubs but now has twenty other outlets in the area while its own distribution company, Flying Firkin, wholesales beer nationwide. Local spring water with Halcyon malts and Fuggles, Northdown and Styrian Goldings hops give the beers a rich malty, fruity and bitter character. They can be enjoyed in the unspoilt, whitewashed Sun with its beams, coal fires and old photos on the walls. T'Owd Tup ale is a dialect expression for an old ram.

BEERS: Bitter, Ramsbottom Strong Ale and T'Owd Tup.

HESKET NEWMARKET

Hesket Newmarket Brewery wears its heart on its sleeve, naming most of its beers after local Cumbrian mountains and fells, but admitting, in the name of Great Cockup Porter, that the beer wasn't meant to look or taste the way it does, while Doris's 90th Birthday Ale is quite simply that: a beer brewed to mark the notable anniversary of the mother of the landlady of the Old Crown pub that fronts the brewery. The brewery was set up by Jim Fearnley in 1988 in a barn behind the Old Crown in a village in the northern Lakes. The beers are wonderfully rich, full-bodied and tangy from hops that include the German variety Hallertauer. They can be enjoyed in the pub with its old church pews where the food is highly recommended, especially the home-made curries.

BEERS: Great Cockup Porter, Blencathra Bitter, Skiddaw Special Bitter, Doris's 90th Birthday Ale, Catbells Pale Ale and Old Carrock Strong Ale.

JENNINGS

Jennings enjoys one of the finest settings of any British brewery. It stands alongside the River Derwent and at the foot of Cockermouth Castle in a small country town that was the birthplace of Fletcher Christian, who led the mutiny on the *Bounty*. The spacious brewery, with whitewashed rooms and its own spring for brewing liquor, was established in 1828 and moved to its present site in 1874. It has an array of traditional mash tuns, coppers and fermenters that use pale and coloured malts with Challenger, Fuggles and Goldings whole flower hops. Jennings owns more than 100 pubs and supplies a further 200 free trade accounts. Its Sneck Lifter ale, close to a porter in style, takes its name from a local dialect expression: a sneck is the latch on a pub door that needs to be lifted before you can enter and order a beer. In winter 1998 Jennings announced a £1 million investment in the brewery to expand production.

BEERS: Dark Mild, Bitter, Cumberland Ale, Cocker Hoop and Sneck Lifter with several seasonal ales.

LEES

John Willie Lees founded his brewery in 1828 at Middleton Junction between Rochdale and Oldham and, with its green gate entrance, cobbled yard, coopers' shop and tall, wonky chimney, it retains a rural air. The company is still owned and run by members of the Lees family and they have a great commitment to cask ales fashioned in a superb brewhouse which is packed with traditional vessels. Much of the beer is still delivered to the brewery's 175 pubs in oak casks, which are repaired by on-site coopers. The beers, with a robust fruity character from the house yeast, are made simply from Maris Otter malt and Goldings hops. Lees is famous for two strong ales: the 7.5 per cent Moonraker, which takes its name from a story about intoxicated farm labourers attempting to rake the reflection of the moon in a pond, while the annual vintage Harvest Ale weighs in at 11.5 per cent alcohol and will improve with age in bottle.

BEERS: GB Mild, Bitter, Moonraker and Harvest Ale. Harvest Ale is brewed every autumn and is available in cask and bottle. Several seasonal and occasional ales are also brewed.

SADDLEWORTH

Julian Taylor brews in stone buildings behind the Church Inn on the site of a former brewery that closed around 130 years ago. Julian was taught the beer-making skills by a former brewer from the long-closed London giant, Charrington. Using a tiny five-barrel plant, Julian uses Maris Otter pale malt with crystal, amber, chocolate and wheat malts for colour and flavour. His hops are Fuggles and Goldings with some American Cascade in some of the brews, hops that give a pronounced citrus/grapefruit aroma and flavour. One of his recent brews, Ayrton's Ale, brewed to commemorate the birth of his son, is a fruit beer in which he uses strawberries and blackberries. The beers are available only in the Church Inn, a stone pub at the head of a valley overlooking Uppermill village.
BEERS: Saddleworth More, Hop Smacker, Ayrton's Ale and Christmas Carol. Shaftbender is brewed for the local Morris Men team.

YATES

Peter and Carole Yates set up their small brewery in 1986 in old farm buildings on their smallholding. Peter had been a professional brewer in Manchester and retired to Cumbria but soon got the brewing bug again. A herd of pedigree goats on the farm develop well on the spent grain and used hops from the brewhouse. The Yateses brew around thirty-four barrels of beer a week, own one pub and supply two dozen others in the locality. Peter Yates helped out the Coniston brewery in 1998 when it won the Champion Beer of Britain competition with Bluebird Bitter and found it hard to cope with demand. At the end of the year, the Yateses decided to retire and sold the brewery to Graeme and Caroline Baxter, former owners of High Force in Co. Durham. BEERS: Bitter, Premium and Best Cellar with a Christmas beer.

Scotland

THE BORDER BETWEEN England and Scotland serves to mark an important divide between the beer styles of the two countries. Brewing developed much later in Scotland than in England due to the consumption of whisky by the masses and imported French wine by the aristocracy as a result of the Auld Alliance. Brewing, when it did develop, reflected the climate and the countryside. Beer had to sustain as well as refresh. Hops were used sparingly as they had to be bought from the English while dark and roasted malts were used generously to give ales body and nourishment. Scotland is a major barley-growing region and the grain grown in the Lowlands is ideal for brewing, whereas the barley that battles through harsh winters further north is better suited to whisky distilling. While Edinburgh in the nineteenth century became an important city for pale ale brewing, with water similar to that of Burton-on-Trent, elsewhere the tradition for darker and roasted beers survived. After years of decline and domination by two Scottish giants, brewing flourishes again in Scotland thanks to the dogged perseverance of new craft breweries from the Lowlands to the Islands. And the Borders are home to Traquair House, the last stately home in the whole of Britain to brew on a regular basis and which in the past has offered refreshment to Mary Queen of Scots and Prince Charles Edward Stuart.

The Borders is a region of wooded valleys and fast-running streams, dotted by small craggy towns and villages. It has literary links with Sir Walter Scott and John Buchan. Further north, once away from the great conurbations of Edinburgh and Glasgow, Scotland becomes sparsely populated, dominated by the magnificent scenery of the Highlands with its mountains and lochs. With brewing mainly confined to the south, the north is home to celebrated whisky distilleries. 'Uisge beatha' or water of life has close links with brewing. Brewers make an unhopped ale with a mash of malted barley, ferment the wort and then distil the alcohol.

BELHAVEN

Brewing in the picturesque seaside town of Dunbar has been taking place since the fourteenth century when monks made ale on the site of what is now the Belhaven Brewery. It is housed in old maltings buildings that have been mellowed by age and smoke. The brewhouse is modern and multi-functional, able to brew both ale and lager. But Belhaven is best known for its cask beers. The 80 Shilling Ale is considered to be the classic of the style (the term shilling comes from a nineteenth-century method of invoicing beer according to strength, from 60 shillings upwards). Belhaven's 80 Shilling is brewed from Pipkin pale, black and crystal malts with Fuggles and Goldings hops and has an aroma of rich malt, toasted grain, hops and gooseberry fruit, with juicy malt and tart hops in the mouth, and a long, dry malty finish with more hints of gooseberry. The brewery also produces a 90 Shilling winter ale that, in bottled form, is labelled Fowler's Wee Heavy. St Andrew's Ale takes its name from a Scottish victory over the English near Dunbar when the flag of St Andrew magically appeared in the sky over the battlefield. The ale named Sandy Hunter is in honour of a legendary former head brewer who still lives in a 'grace-and-favour' house in the grounds. BEERS: 60 Shilling Ale, 70 Shilling Ale, Sandy Hunter's Traditional Ale, 80 Shilling Ale and St Andrew's Ale plus 90 Shilling/Wee Heavy in winter.

BORVE

A tiny brewery tucked away in a remote part of the Scottish Grampians, Borve started life on the Isle of Lewis in 1983 but struggled to sell cask-conditioned ales on an island dominated by the giant Scottish brewers and their keg brands. The tiny plant was moved to the mainland five years later by father-and-son owners Jim and Gregory Hughes and is now housed in former school buildings: another part of the school acts as the brewery tap and visitor centre. The beers are well crafted, using pale and dark malts plus, in the Scottish style, a touch of roasted barley. A complex hop blend includes Omega, Target and German Hersbrucker varieties. The draught beers are hard to find and they are all sold in bottle-fermented form as well.

BEERS: Borve Ale, Tall Ships IPA, Aberdeen Union Street 200 plus Extra Strong, available only in bottle-fermented form.

BROUGHTON

The Broughton brewery was founded in 1979 by David Younger, a member of the famous Scottish brewing clan that, with the McEwans, created the giant Scottish and Newcastle group. Broughton is on a smaller scale in single-storey buildings overlooking fields and sheep. The village of Broughton is best known for its associations with the adventure writer John Buchan and the brewery's Greenmantle Ale is named after one of Buchan's Richard Hannay novels. With Younger's brewing background, the brewhouse is highly professional with traditional mashing, boiling and fermenting vessels. The company was bought in 1995 by Giles Litchfield, owner of the Whim brewery in Derbyshire, who has busily expanded the range of beers. Broughton owns one pub, supplies around 200 outlets in Scotland and sells half its production in bottled form. It has a sizeable export market, including North America. Scottish Oatmeal Stout is a classic of the style, developed as a smoother, creamier and less bitter alternative to dry Irish stout.

BEERS: Bramling Cross, IPA, Greenmantle Ale, Special Bitter, Merlin's Ale, 80 Shilling, Scottish Oatmeal Stout, The Ghillie, Black Douglas and Old Jock.

HARVIESTOUN

Harviestoun has a delightful setting on the edge of the small town of Dollar, based in a 200-year-old stone farm byre at the foot of the Ochil Hills. Ken Brooker is from far-away Essex and came to work in Scotland for the Ford Motor Company. He was a keen home brewer and decided to swap motors for mash tuns in 1985. The success of his beers, which have true Scottish recipes and flavours with a touch more bitterness than is usual, prompted the installation of a new custom-built brewhouse in 1991. Ken and his wife Ingrid now supply around seventy pubs in the area and distribute nationally through wholesalers. Harviestoun achieved greater fame with its Schiehallion cask-conditioned lager (named after a local mountain), which has twice won the top award in the special beer category of the Champion Beer of Britain competition. It is made in the proper continental manner, using imported pale lager malt, a lager yeast culture and Hersbrucker hops from Bavaria. The beer is cold fermented and stored for several months. The ales are made from Pipkin pale and coloured malts with Fuggles, Goldings and Progress whole flower hops. A bottling line has been installed and some of the beers are due to appear in bottle-fermented form.

BEERS: Waverley 70 Shilling, Original 80 Shilling, Montrose Ale, Ptarmigan, Schiehallion and Old Manor plus many occasional and seasonal ales.

ISLE OF SKYE

Isle of Skye brought cask-conditioned beer to an island that lost the tradition decades ago and is better known for its whisky distillery. In this remote part of Scotland, the brewery pays its respects to the Gaelic language by also calling the brewery Leann an Eilein, which means Ales from the Island. The company was set up in 1995 by two schoolteachers at Portree High School, the island's secondary school. The brewery is in custom-built buildings at Uig, the ferry terminal for the Outer Hebrides. Angus MacRuary, one of the founders, now runs the brewery with head brewer Eric Jones. At first, the beers were sold only in a couple of island hotels but they are now distributed throughout Scotland. The Sligachan Hotel on Skye is one of the biggest outlets for cask beer on the west coast of Scotland. Pure water from the island hills is used with the finest malt and hops and there are no artificial ingredients in the beers. A bottling hall was added in 1998. Young Pretender was brewed to commemorate the 250th anniversary of the end of the Jacobite Rebellion in 1746: Prince Charles Edward Stuart (Bonnie Prince Charlie) famously sailed to Skye as a fugitive following the defeat of his army at Culloden. Black Cuillin is named after the main mountain range on Skye while Red Cuillin takes its name from the red hills of the island..
BEERS: Young Pretender, Red Cuillin, Black Cuillin and Avalanche in winter.

ORKNEY

Roger White, a civil engineer from England, set up his small brewery in an old schoolhouse in an isolated part of Orkney in 1988. The Orkadians, used to cold pressurized beers, did not immediately take to his cask ales and he had to find outlets on the mainland. This he did with considerable success, especially when the giant Carlsberg-Tetley group agreed to wholesale the beers. A new brewhouse was built in 1995 to cope with demand. The beers are notably rich, full-bodied and fruity from the use of Golden Promise Scottish barley malts with Challenger, Goldings and Omega hop varieties. Skullsplitter (8.5 per cent) pays bibulous homage to the Vikings who raided the Orkneys. Roger White has experimented with a Bere Ale made from a prehistoric variety of barley that still grows on Orkney and is milled to make the local speciality bran cakes.
BEERS: Northern Light, Raven Ale, Dragonhead Stout, The Red MacGregor, Dark Island and Skullsplitter plus several seasonal ales.

TOMINTOUL

A tiny brewery set up in an old watermill in 1993 on the edge of the highest village in Scotland, Tomintoul is regularly cut off by snow in winter. The company has been successful in finding outlets and now supplies eighty bars and hotels in the Highlands while wholesalers take them as far afield as England and Northern Ireland. The beers are fashioned from Pipkin pale and coloured malts and are hopped with Challenger, Fuggles and Goldings varieties. Many of Scotland's best-known whisky distilleries are also in the area, including the Glenlivet.

BEERS: Laird's Ale, Stag, Nessie's Monster Mash, Culloden and Wild Cat, plus several occasional and seasonal ales. Stag is also available in bottle-fermented form.

TRAQUAIR

Traquair is a magical place, the oldest inhabited stately home in Scotland. With its white-faced and turreted buildings it has the air of an old French château. The 'quair' in the name is an ancient Scottish word for a burn or stream and the one at Traquair not only supplies water for brewing but runs into the River Tweed which marks the boundary between England and Scotland. Mary Queen of Scots stayed at the house and Prince Charles Edward Stuart visited to raise support for the Jacobite cause. The house is owned by the Maxwell Stuarts, members of the Stuart clan, and they keep the main Bear Gates to the house locked until a Stuart returns to the throne. Parts of Traquair House date from the twelfth century. It was rebuilt in the seventeenth century, when a brewhouse, which may be much older, was added to supply the family and servants. A copper was added in 1738. At some time the brewhouse became disused and was discovered in 1965 when Peter Maxwell Stuart became the laird (or lord) of Traquair and found the vessels when he was clearing centuries of jumble from some

outbuildings. As the house is open to the public, the laird was keen to supply visitors with a house ale. With the help of Sandy Hunter from Belhaven Brewery, Maxwell Stuart started to make small batches of bottled beer that soon became both successful and famous, and were exported to the United States and Japan. When he died, his daughter, Lady Catherine Maxwell Stuart, took over the running of house and brewery and has added some modern vessels to cope with demand. At 7.2 per cent, Traquair House Ale is typical of the strong ales once brewed throughout Scotland and which were much admired by French émigrés who escaped the guillotine: they described the rich, amber ales as 'Scottish Burgundy'. The house beer is brewed from pale malt with a touch of black malt and is hopped exclusively with Goldings. It is fermented in oak vessels. Some five outlets take the brewery's regular cask ale, Bear Ale, including the Traquair Arms in the nearby town of Innerleithen.

BEERS: Bear Ale, Traquair House Ale and Jacobite Ale.

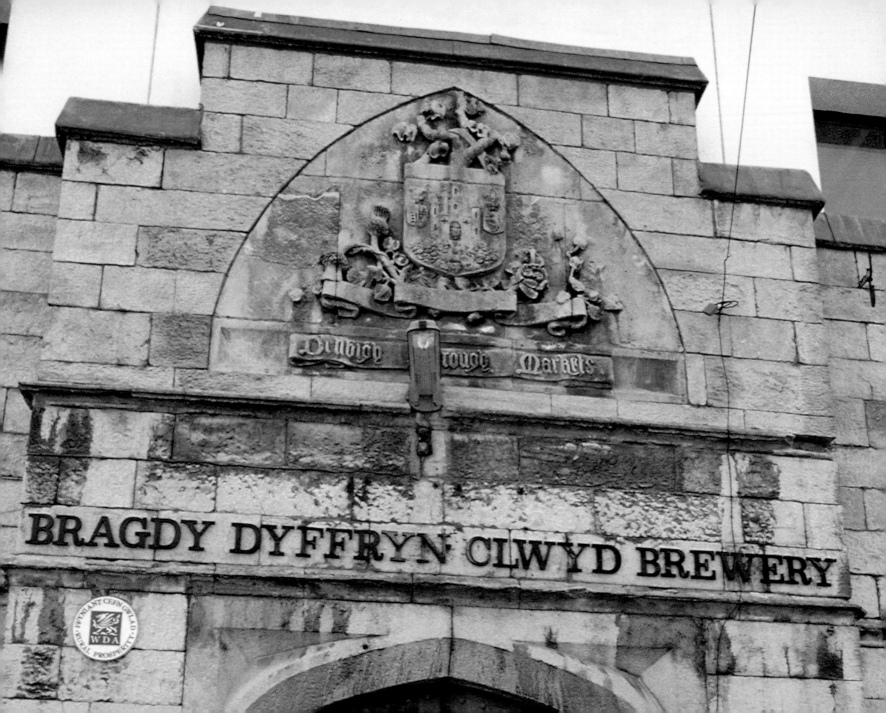

Denbigh Borough Markets

BRAGDY DYFFRYN CLWYD BREWERY

WALES

WALES HAS A LONG TRADITION of brewing handed down from Druids and monks. Centuries ago, powerful ales spiced with herbs, fruit and plants offered solace and refreshment in a harsh and mountainous terrain. In modern times, the demands of miners and steelworkers in the Valleys and central Wales meant that brewers concentrated on dark milds and light bitters to give instant refreshment. The opposition of the Chapel and a powerful temperance movement in the first half of the century meant that most beers were low in strength in order to keep people from the path of drunkenness. South Wales, because of its large captive market, became dominated by large English brewers, but a wider choice can be found at Felinfoel, with its proud use of the Welsh Red Dragon as a logo. Further north, in the Welsh-speaking area, Dyffryn Clwyd offers some rich-tasting, bilingugal ales.

As a result of construction work, it was not possible to photograph the new Tomos Watkin Brewery for this book. Based in Llandeilo, the new craft brewery has rapidly become a force in Welsh brewing. It is owned by Simon Buckley, formerly of the family-owned Buckleys of Llanelli. He has taken the name of a brewery in Llandovery which stopped production in 1928. Tomos Watkin now supplies more than fifty pubs in the area; the brewery was being expanded at the end of 1998, and bottle-fermented beers were being added to the range. A craft centre is attached to the brewery, which owns seven pubs and plans to buy more.

Wales is effectively two countries, divided between the valleys of the south – once dominated by mines and steelworks – with the great cities of Cardiff and Swansea, and the north, with its sparse population and rugged mountains, dotted by small towns where the people are bilingual and in some case speak only Welsh.

DYFFRYN CLYWD

The small brewery was founded in 1994 by a local pub landlord Ioan Evans in a spacious, cool, stone-built former buttery in Denbigh. The brewing vessels are on two storeys and use Halcyon pale and coloured malts with Challenger and Styrian Goldings hops. The beers, some with bilingual names, are sold in pubs in North Wales and into England. The beers have full-bodied flavours with biscuity malt and citric fruit from the hops.
BEERS: Dr Johnson's Draught, Drovers Special Ale/Cwrw Arbennig Porthmon, Special Ale and Four Thumbs/Pedwar Bawd.

FELINFOEL

A village brewery just outside Llanelli, Felinfoel is one of the few surviving breweries in west Wales. It was built in 1878 by David John when the local brewpub was unable to cope with demand. The brewery is still family owned and concentrates on cask ale for its eighty pubs. It is famous for its Double Dragon premium bitter, using the Welsh national emblem as its logo, and in the 1930s for being the first brewery in the world to put beer into tin cans. This was done to help the hard-pressed local tin plate industry during an economic recession. Felinfoel brews with Pipkin pale malt and Challenger, Bramling Cross and Goldings hops.
BEERS: Bitter, Dark and Double Dragon.

MAP OF BREWERY LOCATIONS

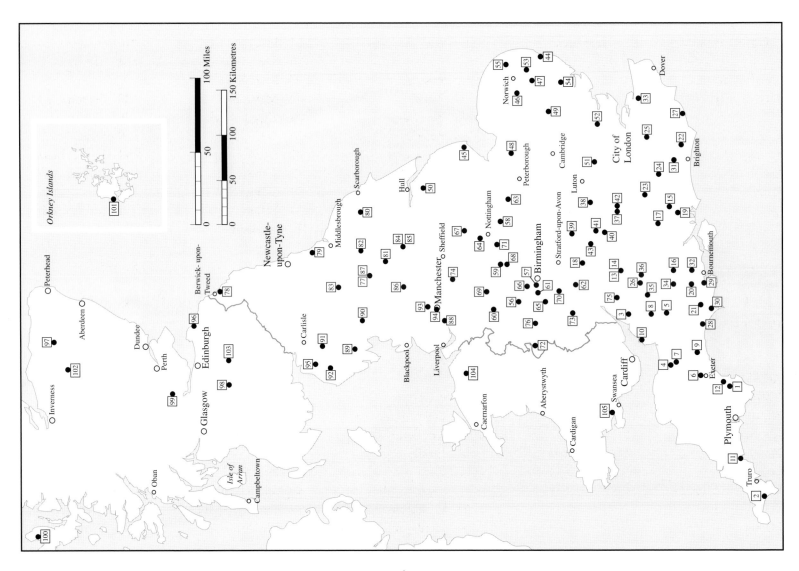

100 Miles

150 Kilometres

Orkney Islands

101

Peterhead

Aberdeen

Inverness

102

97

Dundee

Perth

Edinburgh

96

103

Glasgow

98

99

Oban

Isle of Arran

Campbeltown

100

Berwick-upon-Tweed

78

Newcastle-upon-Tyne

Carlisle

95

91

89

92

Middlesbrough

79

Scarborough

80

82

77 87

83

90

Hull

45

50

Blackpool

Liverpool

104

Manchester

Sheffield

81

84 85

86

93 94 88

Nottingham

67

64

59

60

76

73

72

Aberystwyth

Cardigan

Caernarfon

Swansea

105

Cardiff

4

7

9

6

12

Exeter

1

11

Truro

2

58

63

48

Peterborough

Cambridge

51

Luton

38

39

41

40

43

18

62

65

13

75

57

61

71

68

66

69

70

56

74

Birmingham

Stratford-upon-Avon

37 42

14

26

35

34

8

5

20

21

28

30

29

Bournemouth

10

3

16

32

36

24

23

17

15

19

31

22

25

City of London

52

49

46

44

53

55

47

54

Norwich

33

Dover

27

Brighton

Plymouth

148

Key

West Country

1 Blackawton
2 Blue Anchor
3 Butcombe
4 Cotleigh
5 Cottage
6 Exe Valley
7 Exmoor
8 Oakhill
9 Otter
10 RCH
11 St Austell
12 Teignworthy

Southern England

13 Archers
14 Arkells
15 Ballard's
16 Bunce's
17 Cheriton
18 Donnington
19 Gale's
20 Hall & Woodhouse
21 Thomas Hardy
22 Harveys

23 Hogs Back
24 King & Barnes
25 Larkins
26 Mole's
27 Old Forge
28 Palmer's
29 Poole
30 Quay
31 Rectory
32 Ringwood
33 Shepherd Neame
34 Tisbury
35 Ushers
36 Wadworth

Thames Valley

37 Brakspear
38 Chiltern
39 Hook Norton
40 Morland
41 Morrells
42 Old Luxters
43 Wychwood

Eastern England

44 Adnams
45 Batemans
46 Blue Moon
47 Buffy's
48 Elgood
49 Greene King
50 Highwood
51 McMullen
52 Ridley
53 St Peter's
54 Tolly Cobbold
55 Woodforde's

Heart of England

56 All Nations
57 Batham
58 Belvoir
59 Burton Bridge
60 The Eccleshall Brewery
61 Enville
62 Farmers Arms
   Mayhem's Brew House
63 Grainstore
64 Hardys and Hansons

65 Hobsons
66 Sarah Hughes
67 Mansfield
68 Marston's
69 Shugborough
70 Teme Valley
71 John Thompson
72 Three Tuns
73 Wheatsheaf Inn
74 Whim
75 Wickwar
76 Wood

Yorkshire and North-east England

77 Black Sheep
78 Border
79 Castle Eden
80 Cropton
81 Daleside
82 Hambleton
83 High Force
84 John Smith
85 Samuel Smith
86 Timothy Taylor
87 Theakston

North-west England and the Lakes

88 Burtonwood
89 Coniston
90 Dent
91 Hesket Newmarket
92 Jennings
93 Lees
94 Saddleworth
95 Yates

Scotland

96 Belhaven
97 Borve
98 Broughton
99 Harviestoun
100 Isle of Skye
101 Orkney
102 Tomintoul
103 Traquair

Wales

104 Dyffryn Clwyd
105 Felinfoel

Brewery Addresses

West Country

BLACKAWTON BREWERY, Washbourne, Totnes, Devon TQ9 7UF.
Tel: 01803 732339
Brewery tours not available.

BLUE ANCHOR, 50 Coinagehall Street, Helston, Cornwall TR13 8EX.
Tel: 01326 562821
Brewery tours are available.

BUTCOMBE BREWERY, Butcombe, Bristol BS18 6XQ.
Tel: 01275 472240
Brewery tours are not available.

COTLEIGH BREWERY, Ford Road, Wiveliscombe, Somerset TA4 2RE.
Tel: 01984 624086
Brewery tours are available.

COTTAGE BREWING COMPANY, The Old Cheese Dairy, Lovington, Castle Cary, Somerset BA7 7PS.
Tel: 01963 240551
Brewery tours are available.

EXE VALLEY BREWERY, Land Farm, Silverton, Exeter, Devon EX5 4HF.
Tel: 01392 860406
Brewery tours by arrangement.

.

EXMOOR ALES, Golden Hill Brewery, Wiveliscombe, Somerset TA4 2NY.
Tel: 01984 623798
Brewery tours by arrangement.

OAKHILL BREWERY, The Old Maltings, High Street, Oakhill, Somerset BA3 5BX.
Tel: 01749 840134
Brewery tours by arrangement.

OTTER BREWERY, Mathayes Farm, Luppitt, Honiton, Devon EX14 0SA.
Tel: 01404 891285
Brewery tours by arrangement.

RCH BREWERY, West Hewish, Weston-super-Mare, Somerset BS24 6RR.
Tel: 01934 834447
Brewery tours by arrangement.

ST AUSTELL BREWERY COMPANY, 63 Trevarthian Road, St Austell, Cornwall PL25 4BY.
Tel: 01726 74444
Brewery tours by arrangement.

TEIGNWORTHY BREWERY, The Maltings, Teign Road, Newton Abbot, Devon TQ12 4AA.
Tel: 01626 332066
Brewery tours are not available but Tuckers Maltings is open to visitors.

Southern England

ARCHERS ALES, Penzance Drive, Churchward, Swindon, Wiltshire SN5 7JL.
Tel: 01793 879929
Brewery tours by arrangement. Brewery shop open 9 to 5 Monday to Friday.

ARKELLS' BREWERY, Kingsdown, Swindon, Wiltshire SN2 6RU.
Tel: 01793 823026
Brewery tours by arrangement.

BALLARD'S BREWERY, Unit C, The Old Sawmill, Nyewood, Petersfield, Hampshire GU31 5HA.
Tel: 01730 821301
Brewery tours by arrangement.

BUNCE'S BREWERY, The Old Mill, Netheravon, Salisbury, Wiltshire SP4 9QB.
Tel: 01989 670631
Brewery tours by arrangement.

CHERITON BREWHOUSE, Cheriton, Alresford, Hampshire SO24 0QQ.
Tel: 01962 771166
Brewery tours by arrangement; pub open usual hours.

DONNINGTON BREWERY, Stow-on-the-Wold, Gloucestershire GL54 1EP.
Tel: 01451 830603
Brewery tours are not available.

GEORGE GALE AND CO, The Hampshire Brewery, London Road, Horndean, Hampshire PO8 0DA.
Tel: 01705 571212
Brewery tours by arrangement. Brewery shop open Monday to Friday, 10 to 5.

HALL & WOODHOUSE, The Badger Brewery, Blandford St Mary, Blandford Forum, Dorset DT11 9LS.
Tel: 01258 452141
Brewery tours by arrangement.

THOMAS HARDY BREWERY, Weymouth Avenue, Dorchester DT1 1QT.
Tel: 01305 250255
Brewery tours by arrangement.

HARVEY AND SONS, The Bridge Wharf Brewery, 6 Cliffe High Street, Lewes, East Sussex BN7 2AH.
Tel: 01273 480209
Brewery tours by arrangement (long waiting list).

HOGS BACK BREWERY, Manor Farm, The Street, Tongham, Surrey GU10 1DE.
Tel: 01252 783000
Brewery tours by arrangement. Shop open every day; phone for times.

KING & BARNES, The Horsham Brewery, 18 Bishopric, Horsham, West Sussex RH12 1QP.
Tel: 01403 270470
Brewery tours by arrangement.

LARKINS BREWERY, Larkins Farm, Chiddingstone, Edenbridge, Kent TN8 7BB.
Tel: 01892 870328
Brewery tours by arrangement.

MOLE'S BREWERY, 5 Merlin Way, Bowerhill, Melksham, Wiltshire SN12 6TJ.
Tel: 01225 704734
Brewery tours by arrangement.

Pett Brewing Company, THE OLD FORGE BREWERY, The Two Sawyers, Pett, Hastings, East Sussex TN35 4HB.
Tel: 01424 813030
Brewery tours by arrangement.

J. C. AND R. H. PALMER, The Old Brewery, West Bay, Bridport, Dorset DT6 4JA.
Tel: 01308 422396
Brewery tours by arrangement. Brewery shop open Monday to Saturday.

POOLE BREWERY, The Brewhouse, 68 High Street, Poole, Dorset BH15 1DA.
Tel: 01202 682345
Brewery tours by arrangement.

THE QUAY BREWERY, Hope Square, Weymouth, Dorset DT4 8TR.
Tel: 01305 777515
Shop open Monday to Sunday, 9.30 to 4.30.

RECTORY ALES, Streat Hill Farm, Streat Hill, Streat, Hassocks, West Sussex BN6 8RP.
Tel: 01273 890570
Brewery tours by arrangement.

RINGWOOD BREWERY, Christchurch Road, Ringwood, Hampshire BH24 3AP.
Tel: 01425 471177
Brewery tours by arrangement. Shop open Monday to Saturday.

SHEPHERD NEAME, 17 Court Street, Faversham, Kent ME13 7AX.
Tel: 01795 532206
Brewery tours by arrangement.

TISBURY BREWERY, Church Street, Tisbury, Wiltshire SP3 6NH.
Tel: 01747 870986
Brewery tours by arrangement.

USHERS OF TROWBRIDGE, Directors House, 68 Fore Street, Trowbridge, Wiltshire BA14 8JF.
Tel: 01225 763171
Brewery tours by arrangement.

WADWORTH AND COMPANY, Northgate Brewery, Devizes, Wiltshire SN10 1JW.
Tel: 01380 723361
Brewery tours by arrangement in September only. Shop open normal office hours.

THAMES VALLEY

W. H. BRAKSPEAR AND SONS, The Brewery, New Street, Henley-on-Thames, Oxfordshire RG9 2BU.
Tel: 0141 570200
Brewery tours by arrangement. Shop open Monday to Saturday, 9 to 6.

THE CHILTERN BREWERY, Nash Lee Road, Terrick, Aylesbury, Buckinghamshire HP17 0TQ.
Tel: 01296 613647
Brewery tours by arrangement. Shop open Monday to Saturday 9 to 5.

HOOK NORTON BREWERY COMPANY, Brewery Lane, Hook Norton, Banbury, Oxfordshire OX15 5NY.
Tel: 01608 737210
Brewery tours by arrangement (strictly limited).

MORLAND, The Brewery, Ock Street, Abingdon, Oxfordshire OX14 5BZ.
Tel: 01235 553377
Brewery tours by arrangement.

MORRELLS BREWERY (RIP), The Lion Brewery, St Thomas's Street, Oxford OX1 1LA.
Brewery tours no longer available.

OLD LUXTERS FARM BREWERY, Hambleden, Henley-on-Thames, Oxfordshire RG9 6JW.
Tel: 01491 638330 (Farm signposted from A4155 Henley to Marlow road.)
Brewery tours by arrangement. Shop open seven days a week.

WYCHWOOD BREWERY COMPANY, The Eagle Maltings, The Crofts, Corn Street, Witney, Oxfordshire OX8 7AZ.
Tel: 01993 702574
Brewery tours by arrangement.

EASTERN ENGLAND

ADNAMS AND COMPANY, Sole Bay Brewery, East Green, Southwold, Suffolk IP18 6JW.
Tel: 01502 727200
Brewery tours are not available except for CAMRA groups. Brewery shop open Monday to Friday, 10 to 6.

GEORGE BATEMAN AND SON, Salem Bridge Brewery, Wainfleet, Lincolnshire PE24 4JE.
Tel: 017754 880317
Brewery tours by arrangement. Shop open Monday to Friday, 9 to 5.

BLUE MOON BREWERY, Pearces Farm, Seamere, Hingham, Norfolk NR9 4LP.
Tel: 01953 851625
Brewery tours by arrangement.

BUFFY'S BREWERY, Mardle Hall, Rectory Road, Tivetshall St Mary, Norfolk NR15 2DD.
Tel: 01379 676523
Brewery tours by arrangement.

ELGOOD AND SONS, North Brink Brewery, Wisbech, Cambridgeshire PE13 1LN.
Tel: 01945 583160
Brewery and garden trips by arrangement.

GREENE KING, Westgate Brewery, Westgate Street, Bury St Edmunds, Suffolk IP33 1QT.
Tel: 01284 763222 Brewery tours by arrangement.

HIGHWOOD BREWERY, Melton Highwood, Barnetby, Lincolnshire DN38 6AA.
Tel: 01652 680020
Brewery tours by arrangement.

McMULLEN AND SONS, The Hertford Brewery, 26 Old Cross, Hertford SG14 1RD.
Tel: 01992 584911
Brewery tours by arrangement.

T. D. RIDLEY AND SONS, Hartford End Brewery, Felsted, Chelmsford, Essex CM3 1JZ.
Tel: 01371 820316
Brewery tours by arrangement.

ST PETER'S BREWERY, St Peter's Hall, St Peter South Elmham, Bungay, Suffolk NR35 1NQ.
Tel: 01986 782322
Brewery tours by arrangement.

TOLLEMACHE AND COBBOLD BREWERY, Cliff Road, Ipswich, Suffolk IP3 0AZ.
Tel: 01473 231723
Daily brewery trips for groups available. Brewery shop open lunchtime in tourist season.

WOODFORDE'S NORFOLK ALES, Broadland Brewery, Woodbastwick, Norfolk NR13 6SW.
Tel: 01603 720353
Brewery tours by arrangement.

HEART OF ENGLAND

ALL NATIONS, Coalport Road, Madeley, Shropshire TF7 5DP.
Tel: 01952 585747
Brewery tours not usually available. Pub open normal hours.

DANIEL BATHAM AND SON, Delph Brewery, Delph Road, Brierley Hill, West Midlands DY5 2TN.
Tel: 01384 77229
Brewery tours are not available. Pub open usual hours.

BELVOIR BREWERY, Woodhill, Nottingham Lane, Old Dalby, Leicestershire LE 14 3LX.
Tel: 01664 823455
Brewery tours by arrangement.

BURTON BRIDGE BREWERY, 24 Bridge Street, Burton-on-Trent, Staffordshire DE14 1SY
Tel: 01283 510573
Brewery tours by arrangement. Pub open usual hours.

SLATERS ECCLESHALL BREWERY, George Hotel, Castle Street, Eccleshall, Staffordshire ST21 6DF.
Tel: 01785 850300
Brewery tours by arrangement.

ENVILLE ALES, Enville Brewery, Cox Green, Enville, Staffordshire DY7 5LG.
Tel: 01384 873728
Brewery tours by arrangement.

FARMERS ARMS MAYHEM'S BREW HOUSE, Lower Apperley, Gloucestershire GL19 4DR.
Tel: 01452 780307
Brewery tours by arrangement. Pub open usual hours.

Davis'es Brewing Company, THE GRAINSTORE BREWERY, Station Approach, Oakham, Rutland LE15 6QW.
Tel: 01572 770065
Brewery tours by arrangement. Tap room open usual pub hours.

HARDYS AND HANSONS, Kimberley Brewery, Kimberley, Nottinghamshire NG16 2NS.
Tel: 0115 938 3611
Brewery tours by arrangement

HOBSONS BREWERY, Newhouse Farm, Tenbury Road, Cleobury Mortimer, Worcestershire DY14 8DP.
Tel: 01299 270837
Brewery tours by arrangement.

SARAH HUGHES BREWERY, Beacon Hotel, 129 Bilston Street, Sedgley, West Midlands DY3 1JE.
Tel: 01902 883380
Brewery tours by arrangement. Hotel bars open usual hours.

MANSFIELD BREWERY, Littleworth, Mansfield, Nottinghamshire NG18 1AB.
Tel: 01623 25691
Brewery tours by arrangement.

MARSTON, THOMPSON AND EVERSHED, Shobnall Road, Burton-on-Trent, Staffordshire DE14 2BW.
Tel: 01283 531131
Brewery tours by arrangement. Shop open 10 to 2.

SHUGBOROUGH
All enquiries to Titanic Brewery, Unit G, Harvey Works, Lingard Street, Burslem, Stoke-on-Trent, Staffordshire ST6 1ED.
Tel: 01782 823447
Brewery tours by arrangement.

TEME VALLEY BREWERY, The Talbot at Knightwick, Knightwick, Worcestershire WR6 5HP.
Tel: 01886 821235
Brewery tours by arrangement. Pub open usual hours.

JOHN THOMPSON BREWERY/LLOYDS COUNTRY BEERS, John Thompson Inn, Ingleby, near Melbourne, Derbyshire DE7 1NW.
Tel: 01332 863426
Brewery tours by arrangement.

THREE TUNS, Salop Street, Bishop's Castle, Shropshire SY9 5BW.
Tel: 01588 638023.
Brewery tours by arrangement. Pub open usual hours.

WHEATSHEAF INN AND FROMES HILL BREWERY, Fromes Hill, near Ledbury, Herefordshire HR8 1HT.
Tel: 01531 64088
Brewery tours by arrangement.

WHIM ALES, Whim Farm, Hartington, Buxton, Derbyshire SK17 0AX.
Tel: 01298 84991
Brewery tours by arrangement.

WICKWAR BREWING COMPANY, Arnolds Cooperage, The Old Cider Mill, Station Road, Wickwar, Gloucestershire GL12 8NB.
Tel: 01454 294168
Brewery tours by arrangement.

WOOD BREWERY, Wistanstow, Craven Arms, Shropshire SY7 8DG.
Tel: 01588 672523
Brewery tours by arrangement but strictly limited; visitor centre planned. Pub open usual hours.

YORKSHIRE AND NORTH-EAST ENGLAND

BLACK SHEEP BREWERY, Wellgarth, Masham, North Yorkshire HG4 3EN.
Tel: 01765 689227
Brewery tours by arrangement. Shop, bistro and visitor centre open daily.

BORDER BREWERY COMPANY, The Old Kiln, Brewery Lane, Tweedmouth, Berwick-upon-Tweed, Northumberland TD15 2AH.
Tel: 01289 303303
Brewery tours by arrangement.

CASTLE EDEN BREWERY, Castle Eden, Co. Durham TS27 4SX.
Tel: 01429 836007
Brewery tours by arrangement.

CROPTON BREWERY, Woolcroft, Cropton, near Pickering, North Yorkshire YO18 8HH.
Tel: 01751 417310
Brewery tours available without prior arrangement. Shop 10 to 4 daily.

DALESIDE BREWERY, Camwal Road, Starbeck, Harrogate, North Yorkshire HG1 4PT.
Tel: 01423 880041
Brewery tours are not available.

HAMBLETON ALES, The Brewery, Holme-on-Swale, Thirsk, North Yorkshire YO7 4JE.
Tel: 01845 567460
Brewery tours by arrangement. Shop open Monday to Saturday.

HIGH FORCE HOTEL BREWERY, Forest-in-Teesdale, Barnard Castle, Co. Durham DL12 0XH.
Tel: 01833 622222
Brewery tours by arrangement. Hotel bar open usual hours.

JOHN SMITH, The Brewery, Tadcaster, North Yorkshire LS24 9SA.
Tel: 01937 832091.
Brewery tours by arrangement.

SAMUEL SMITH, The Old Brewery, High Street, Tadcaster, North Yorkshire LS24 9SB.
Tel: 01937 83225
Brewery tours by arrangement.

TIMOTHY TAYLOR, Knowle Spring Brewery, Keighley, West Yorkshire BD21 1AW.
Tel: 01535 603139
Brewery tours are not available.

T. & R. THEAKSTON, Wellgarth, Masham, Ripon, North Yorkshire HG4 4YD.
Tel: 01765 689544
Brewery tours and shop available daily.

NORTH-WEST ENGLAND AND THE LAKES

BURTONWOOD BREWERY, Bold Lane, Burtonwood, Warrington, Cheshire WA5 4PJ.
Tel: 01925 225131
Brewery tours by arrangement.

CONISTON BREWING COMPANY, Coppermines Road, Coniston, Cumbria LA21 8HL.
Tel: 01539 441133
Brewery tours by arrangement. Pub open usual hours.

DENT BREWERY, Hollins, Cowgill, Dent, Cumbria LA10 5TQ.
Tel: 01539 625326
Brewery tours by arrangement. Pub open usual hours

HESKET NEWMARKET BREWERY, Old Crown Barn, Back Green, Hesket Newmarket, Cumbria CA7 8JG.
Tel: 016974 78066
Brewery tours by arrangement. Pub open usual hours.

JENNINGS BROTHERS, The Castle Brewery, Cockermouth, Cumbria CA13 9NE.
Tel: 01900 823214
Brewery tours by arrangement. Shop open Monday to Friday 9 to 4.45.

J. W. LEES AND COMPANY, Greengate Brewery, Middleton Junction, Greater Manchester M24 2AX.
Tel: 0161 643 2487
Brewery tours by arrangement.

SADDLEWORTH, Church Inn, Uppermill, Saddleworth, Greater Manchester OL3 6LW.
Tel: 01457 820902
Brewery tours by arrangement

YATES BREWERY, Ghyll Farm, Westnewton, Aspatria, Cumbria CA5 3NX.
Tel: 016973 21081
Brewery tours are not available.

SCOTLAND

BELHAVEN BREWERY, Spott Road, Dunbar, Lothian EH42 1RS.
Tel: 01368 862734
Brewery tours by arrangement

BORVE BREW HOUSE, Ruthven by Huntly, Moray, Grampian AB54 4SG.
Tel: 01466 760343
Brewery tours by arrangement. Pub hours limited: phone for details.

BROUGHTON ALES, The Brewery, Broughton, Biggar, Borders ML12 6HQ.
Tel: 01899 830345
Brewery tours by arrangement (evenings only). Shop open Monday to Friday 9 to 5.

HARVIESTOUN BREWERY, Devon Road, Dollar, Clackmannanshire FK14 7LX.
Tel: 01259 742141
Brewery tours are not available.

ISLE OF SKYE BREWING COMPANY/LEANN AN EILEIN, The Pier, Uig, Isle of Skye IV51 9XY.
Tel: 01470 542477
Brewery tours by arrangement.

THE ORKNEY BREWERY, Quoyloo, Stromness, Sandwick, Orkney KW16 3LT.
Tel: 01856 841802
Brewery tours by arrangement.

TOMINTOUL BREWERY COMPANY, Mill of Auchriachan, Tomintoul, Banffshire AB37 9EQ.
Tel: 01807 580333
Brewery tours are not available.

TRAQUAIR HOUSE BREWERY, Traquair House, Innerleithen, Peeblesshire EH44 6PW.
Tel: 01896 831370
House and brewery tours by arrangement April to October. Shop open daily during the same period.

WALES

BRAGDY DYFFRYN CLWYD (Denbigh Brewery in Clwyd), Chapel Place, Denbigh, Clwyd LL16 3TJ.
Tel: 01745 815007
Brewery tours by arrangement.

FELINFOEL BREWERY COMPANY, Farmers Row, Felinfoel, Llanelli, Dyfed SA14 8LB.
Tel: 01554 773357
Brewery tours are not available. Shop open Monday to Friday.

THE CAMPAIGN FOR REAL ALE (CAMRA) supports traditional beers, brewers and pubs and publishes the annual Good Beer Guide.
For details of membership, telephone 01727 867201 or write to CAMRA, 230 Hatfield Road, St Albans, Herts AL1 4LW.

Photographer's Notes

Breweries come in all shapes and sizes, from the magnificent red bricks of Wadworth's to the pink-washed ivy-clad walls of tiny Buffy's. All have brewers who ply their alchemy with mash tun, copper and fermentation vessels to turn barley, hops and water into that magnificent real ale we drink with so much pleasure. I have tried, and hopefully succeeded, in creating a sequence of pictures that reflect the variety of breweries and the mystery of brewing.

Where possible I have tried to omit modern-day distractions, such as cars, road signs, and cables. However, these are working plants, some are over one hundred years old, and through many years of modernization functionality has triumphed over beauty.

For most of my life I have drunk real ales and travelled about this beautiful country and I thought I knew it. But in completing this book I travelled well over 20,000 miles from Cornwall to Kent, Orkney to Skye, to the Borders, and to the other counties of England and Wales and discovered places that I had only dreamt about. The journey from Orkney to Skye was one such trip. First across the sea past the tallest cliffs in these islands, then through the wonderful Scottish wilderness, devoid of people and traffic but with sunlight and clouds chasing each other across the flatlands and mountains. It could not be better.

All the photographs were taken using a Bronica S2A with a standard 80mm lens and Nikon F3s with either 24mm, 28mm or 35–105mm zoom lenses being used dependent on the conditions and the shots that I wanted. All the photographs except two were taken using natural light and an exposure of between one second and a thirtieth of a second; for the other two photographs I used bounced-flash generated from a Metz gun held off the camera. My thanks go to Kodak who just in time brought out E100SW film. I used this film for all the photographs as it gave me the saturation and warmth that I wanted without having to use filters.

Other equipment used included a compass to establish light direction and local Ordnance Survey maps as some of the breweries are well off the beaten track. A step ladder and heavy duty tripod were necessary for height and stability and several good novels and guide books were read while waiting for the right light or the rain to stop. The other piece of equipment that I could not do without is a radio to listen to the weather forecast. I often wondered why it was raining when the forecaster talked about the sunny spells around my area! Sometimes I was lucky and just visited the site once, but often, due to the weather, I needed to visit twice and in one case three times.

The miles driven, the films shot and the hours spent producing this book are my tribute to these wonderful buildings, the country breweries.

ACKNOWLEDGEMENTS

THANKS TO ALL THE BREWERS, owners, assistants and helpers who went out of their way to give me time, support and in many cases muscle to enable me to take the images that I wanted. Their simple devotion to brewing and real ale augurs well for the future. Thanks also to members of the British Guild of Beer Writers for ideas and suggestions. And many thanks to Mole, whose encouragement, scissors, eyes and common sense made my work a vastly pleasurable experience.

Author's Notes

BEER HAS COME to be acknowledged as the national beverage of England. At a recent conference of brewers, Lord Burton claimed that this country owed its high and proud position among the nations of the earth simply on account of its characteristic diet, Beef and Beer. Whereupon someone made the waggish comment, 'Why drag in the Beef?'

F. W. Hackwood, writing in 1910, had no need to convince anyone in England or the whole of Britain of the importance of the country's brewing traditions. Imperial pride and the international acclaim for the India Pale Ales of Burton-on-Trent asserted that British beer was the best in the world. At the turn of a new century, we are no longer so certain. While the British still drink four times as much beer as wine, to read the broadsheet newspapers and watch television food and drink programmes it would be easy to draw the conclusion that we have abandoned beer for the juice of the grape. The British seem no longer to value or acclaim the things we do well. While it would be absurd to suggest that British beer is best, it cannot be denied that the mild and pale ales, porters, stouts, old ales and barley wines produced in this country are a singular contribution to the world of beer, especially when they come half-finished from breweries and reach maturity and perfection in casks in pub cellars due to a natural second fermentation.

The uncertainty about Britain's role as a brewing nation is underscored by the growth of a handful of giant brewing combines that, driven by the demands of the market, their accountants and the need to make quick and easy profits, have largely abandoned the quality and tradition enshrined in cask-conditioned ales in favour of lager and processed and pressurized ales known as 'nitro-keg'. The brewing giants control around 80 per cent of all the beer made and sold in Britain. They dominate the 'free trade' (pubs not owned directly by breweries) by offering large discounts and cheap loans that smaller companies cannot hope to match. The war of attrition waged by the big brewers has taken its toll. The share of the market enjoyed by regional and still largely family-owned breweries fell from 22 per cent to 15 per cent in the 1990s. Some regional breweries have thrown in the towel, abandoning brewing to concentrate on running pub estates with beers supplied by other producers. In the tragic case of Morrells of Oxford, a tawdry struggle to sell the company as quickly as possible for as much cash as possible led to the closure of the last brewery in the university city. As this book was being completed, Britain's biggest regional brewer, Wolverhampton and Dudley, made a £262 million bid for Marston's of Burton-on-Trent. Should that bid succeed it will inevitably encourage other regional brewers to huddle together, merge their resources, and close unnecessary plants in order to face up to the increasingly harsh nature of the modern market place.

This book, if nothing else, is a timely reminder of Britain's proud brewing traditions. It is not merely a nostalgic look at a bucolic past, though a belief in community and serving customers rather than accountants is not an attitude that should be dismissed as old-fashioned or irrelevant to the modern world. The aim of the book is to celebrate what is good in British brewing and to encourage producers both large and small to concentrate on what they do well and produce ales that people rather than accountants want. The situation is not without hope. Compared to most countries, Britain still has a great diversity and choice of beers. And it has a growing number of small but gifted and immensely determined craft brewers to bolster and develop that diversity.

Readers who make the effort to visit the breweries in these pages and sample the beers have a part to play in their future. The Campaign for Real Ale, formed in the early 1970s, now has 53,000 members, continues to battle to save independent brewers and to offer, through hundreds of beer festivals held every year, shop windows for their products. (Details of membership from CAMRA at 230 Hatfield Road, St Albans, Herts AL1 4LW; telephone 01727 867201.)

Together, proud brewers and dedicated beer lovers can ensure that the heritage of country producers celebrated in this book can survive to enrich all our futures.

HEREFORDSHIRE OAST HOUSE

As soon as hops are harvested in the early autumn they are taken to oast houses to be dried. As a result of their high moisture content, hops will turn black and go mouldy within twenty-four hours unless they are dried. In the oast house, the plants are spread out on floors where warm air from heaters dries them. The rotating cowl on the top of the oast house helps keep a good downward draught of air circulating over the hops. When drying is finished, the hops are packed into tall sacks known as 'pockets'. Brewers use either the whole flowers of the hop or compressed pellets.

Hops need rich, well-drained sandy or loamy soil in which to flourish. The principal hop-growing areas of England are Kent, Herefordshire and Worcestershire. Only the female hop is used in brewing. English hops are

fertilized by the male of the species, while hops used predominantly in lager brewing are unfertilized. As a result, English hops give rich spicy, floral, peppery, citrus and resiny aromas and flavours to beer. There are many varieties of hops grown in England. Brewers will often use two or more hops in the brewing process to balance aroma and bitterness: the classic blend of the Fuggle and the Golding allows the brewer to blend the tangy bitterness of the Fuggle with the peppery and spicy character of the Golding.

Hop plants traditionally grow to around sixteen feet but in the late 1990s growers began to develop new varieties of 'dwarf' hops that grow to just eight feet. Such hops are easier to pick and are less prone to disease and attack from pests than traditional varieties. One of the dwarf varieties, First Gold, quickly established itself with brewers due to its good bitterness and aroma.

INDEX